GETTING INTO GRADUATE BUSINESS SCHOOL TODAY

Thomas H. Martinson
and
David P. Waldherr

MACMILLAN • USA

Macmillan General Reference
A Simon & Schuster Macmillan Company
1633 Broadway
New York, NY 10019-6785

An Arco Book

MACMILLAN is a registered trademark of Macmillan, Inc.
ARCO is a registered trademark of Prentice-Hall, Inc.

Library of Congress Cataloging-in-Publication Data

Martinson, Thomas H.
    Getting into graduate business school today / Thomas H. Martinson
and David P. Waldherr.
        p.   cm.
    ISBN 0-02-860620-5 (pbk.)
    1. Business schools—United States. 2. College choice—United
States. 3. Graduate Management Admission Test. I. Waldherr, David
P.
    HF1131.M29   1996
    650'.071'173—dc20   95-35986
                                                                  CIP
Manufactured in the United States of America
10 9 8 7 6 5 4 3 2 1

Book design by A&D Howell

CONTENTS

PREFACE V

INTRODUCTION VII

1. GRADUATE MANAGEMENT STUDY 1

2. INSIDE THE ADMISSIONS OFFICE 15

3. TARGETING SCHOOLS 31

4. ANATOMY OF AN APPLICATION 47

5. THE PERSONAL STATEMENT: WHAT TO SAY 63

6. FIVE PERSONAL STATEMENTS THAT WORKED 85

7. TAKING THE GMAT 107

APPENDIX—AACSB-ACCREDITED SCHOOLS OF BUSINESS ... 127

PREFACE

The title *Getting Into Graduate Business School Today* is not exactly descriptive of the content of this book. The book might more accurately have been entitled *Getting Into a GOOD Business School Today.* Simply "getting into business school," if that phrase means gaining admission to just any school at all, is not really a difficult task because there are over 700 accredited business schools in this country alone; at many schools, the admissions standards are so relaxed that nearly every applicant is accepted. On the other hand, gaining admission to a business school with a decent reputation may be problematic; schools such as Harvard, Kellogg, Sloan, Tuck, and Wharton—to mention just a few big guns—are extremely selective, accepting only one out of five or one out of six applications.

Thus, the parallel between *Getting Into Business School Today* and *Getting Into Law School Today* or *Getting Into Medical School,* other titles in this series, is not exact. Unlike entry into the practice of law or medicine, admission to "business" is not controlled by licensing procedures. Consequently, "business schools" do not have to satisfy any governmental or quasi-governmental criteria to declare themselves eligible to confer on students the Master of Business Administration degree. In a fittingly laissez-faire manner, therefore, the quality of programs offered by business schools runs the gamut from poor to acceptable to good to outstanding.

If you are planning to apply only to a local school for a part-time program that accepts virtually every applicant with even minimal academic credentials, then this book will be of only marginal value to you—although you may find some of the chapters, such as the one that discusses school rankings and the one that discusses preparing for the GMAT, interesting reading. If you are planning to apply to schools with regional reputations, then you will find this book very valuable, for the analysis and suggestions it contains will enable you to maximize your chances for admission at those schools. And if you are setting your sights on first-tier schools with substantial national reputations, then you will find this book absolutely indispensable, for at those most competitive of business schools every aspect of the application is rigorously scrutinized and a wrong choice for a letter of recommendation or an ill-considered response to a question on the application could make the difference between rejection and acceptance.

INTRODUCTION

This is a guide to or a handbook on applying to business school—a "how-to" book, if you will. The objective of this book is generally to help you to approach the business school admissions process in a rational manner and more particularly to help you get into the very best business school for which your credentials qualify you.

Some people may wonder whether a book like this is really needed. After all, it might be suggested that a business-school application is what it is: You take the Graduate Management Admission Test (GMAT), fill in some blanks on a form, arrange for a couple of letters of recommendation, make sure that everything gets to the school's admissions office on time with a check or money order for the application fee, and hope for the best. Could anyone possibly write a book about that? And the answer, of course, is no.

What makes this book valuable is the fact that the business school application process can be immensely more complex than suggested by the preceding paragraph. Consider the first point mentioned: You take the GMAT. The GMAT is a standardized examination given several times each year that is designed to test a candidate's potential for graduate study in management. Virtually all business schools require applicants to take the GMAT, and your performance on this test is likely to have a very large impact on your chance for admission and ultimately upon your career.

You may not be aware of their existence or perhaps are aware of them but simply have not paid much attention to them, but there are schools that offer courses to help candidates prepare for the GMAT. Some of these schools claim that their "coaching" generates substantial score improvement, but they may charge more than $1,000 for their service. Should you enroll at such a school?

You can see that the seemingly simple first step of applying to business school—taking the GMAT—has already become a $1,000 question. Or, to pursue the figure of speech, if it should turn out that a $1,000 coaching course makes the difference between acceptance at a first-tier business school and acceptance at a "second-string" institution, then the item can no longer be considered just a $1,000 question. Instead, it becomes a $10,000, a $100,000, or a $1 million question.

Now consider the second step of the application process mentioned above: Fill in the blanks on an application. The application forms for many business schools, particularly the competitive ones, are considerably more complicated than just a few blanks. Indeed, a highly competitive school, which might receive five or six applications for every available opening, may use a form that is several pages long. Moreover, the information solicited goes far beyond "name and address" or even "employment history." The application form to a top business school may ask for a series of essay responses to questions such as "What are your three most significant weaknesses?" or "In what way do you think an M.B.A. would further your career?" Why are these questions included in an application form? What weight is given to the responses to these questions? What kind of response would be the most effective? Again, you see that the application process is not so simple.

Similarly, other aspects of the admissions process raise important issues. How important are letters of recommendation, and who should write them? What are the best business schools, and what does it take to get accepted? What about interviews? What about "connections"?

And these are only some of the questions that you will have to answer. Fortunately, these questions do have answers, and the applicant who takes the time to learn what they are will have a pronounced competitive advantage over those applicants who do not make the effort. This, then, is the justification for this book: Advance planning, reflective thought, and careful attention to detail can greatly improve your chance of admission to your first-choice school.

GRADUATE
MANAGEMENT STUDY

Let's begin our discussion of the application process with an overview of graduate education in business management.

"B" IS FOR BUSINESS

The letters "M.B.A." stand for Master of Business Administration, the degree that has traditionally been awarded in the field of graduate study in management practices. Although "M.B.A." is the proper name of a particular degree, the letters are also used as a popular shorthand for all degrees awarded in the field of graduate management study, including degrees awarded upon the completion of a traditional M.B.A. curriculum but called by a different name, such as the Master of Management, and degrees awarded for management study in a particular area, such as the Master of Health Administration. Similarly, the phrases "business school" and "B-school" are used generically to refer to any institution that offers graduate programs in management studies, even though some of those programs may focus on activities such as nonprofit organizations that might not ordinarily be considered "business" in the strict sense of commerce.

Since the wider and looser usage of the terms "M.B.A.," "business school," and "B-school" is firmly established, we will take advantage of the simplicity that it offers. We will use "M.B.A" to refer to any graduate degree in management and the terms "business school" and "B-school" to refer to any institution that offers programs of graduate study in management.

VARIATIONS IN B-MAJOR

The prototypical M.B.A. program required two academic years of full-time study and was built around courses such as Accounting, Finance, Personnel Management, and Marketing. Today, there are many variations on this theme. There are programs that allow students to start at the end of or in the middle of the academic year; there are programs that can be completed in three rather than four semesters; there are "executive" or other M.B.A. programs that require even less time and are intended to enhance the management skills of people who already have considerable managerial authority; there are programs that include courses like Health Policy and Not-for-Profit Organizations; and there are programs that award degrees in specific areas such as Health Care or Not-for-Profit Management.

The differences in structure and content of particular programs will obviously be very important to you, and you should spend time studying the various options that are available to you. For the purposes of this book, however, we can ignore these variations. We will speak about the admissions process, as though every reader were applying to a prototypical program. Little, if anything, will be lost by this simplification. The relevant considerations—what factors are taken into account and how to maximize your chances of acceptance—are not all that variable.

"A" IS FOR ACCREDITATION

Although business schools are affiliated with academic institutions, they are primarily organized to provide professional training for students who wish to pursue a career in business (using that term loosely) rather than a career in academia. In this respect, a business school is like a law school. The goal of the program of study is to produce practitioners rather than academicians.

On the other hand, unlike law schools, business schools are not required to meet any governmental standards in order to maintain their status as degree-granting institutions. Indeed, this helps to explain why there are more than 700 institutions in the United States that grant M.B.A.s but only 175 or so that grant law degrees. Additionally, new M.B.A.s are not required to pass a proficiency test like the bar exam before entering on their careers—except those who want a special credential such as the C.P.A.

This does not mean, however, that business schools do not try to meet any minimum standards nor that it is impossible to make judgments about the relative merits of the programs offered by the various schools. At the very least, you will want to make sure that the schools you consider are accredited by one of the six nationally recognized accrediting agencies: the Middle States Association of Colleges and Schools, the New England Association of Schools and Colleges, the North Central Association of Colleges and Schools, the Northwest Association of Schools and Colleges, the Southern Association of Colleges and Schools, or the Western Association of Schools and Colleges. As of this writing, there are more than 700 U.S. colleges and universities with such accreditation that offer M.B.A. programs.

In addition to general institutional accreditation, over 250 business schools have also demonstrated that their programs meet the standards of the American Assembly of Collegiate Schools of Business (AACSB). To qualify for AACSB accreditation, a school has to meet certain minimum standards in areas such as faculty resources and qualifications, curriculum, library facilities, and physical plant. An AACSB accreditation is a further assurance that a school's program provides a well-rounded education including exposure to developing areas such as ethics and international business.

Finally, it is also possible to make some comparative judgments about the quality of the programs offered by various schools. As you will see in chapter 2, factors such as the average or median GMAT score and GPA of a business school's student body and the average or median starting salary of its recent graduates can provide useful, if not entirely perfect, bases for comparison. Each year, in its "college ranking" issue, the magazine *U.S. News and World Report* publishes a listing that compares business schools along these and other dimensions. Additionally, the magazine *Business Week* has prepared a handbook entitled *The Best Business Schools* (published by McGraw-Hill, Inc.). And ARCO, the publisher of the guide you are now using, has published a guide entitled *The Best Graduate Business Schools* (written by Thomas Bachhuber). Chapter 3 will discuss the strengths and weaknesses of these and other similar publications and offer guidance in how to make the best use of them.

THE JOB MARKET

During the 1970s, demand for the M.B.A. increased dramatically, with the number of M.B.A. degrees granted each year more than doubling to about 50,000. Companies were hiring more and more M.B.A.s, and more and more people wanted to have the degree. During this Golden Age of the M.B.A., the degree was seen as a passport to the upper echelon of business—the hot ticket to a corner office and a salary with lots of digits plus plenty of "perks."

More recently, however, there has been a growing disenchantment with the degree. To be sure, the number of M.B.A.s awarded continued to grow through the 1980s (to a total of about 75,000 each year by the end of the decade). But the early 1990s saw a decline in the number of candidates taking the Graduate Management Admission Test, a fact that has been interpreted as a sign of a decrease in interest in M.B.A. programs. Certainly, there is a growing sense that the degree is no longer the "greased slide" to professional success that it once seemed to be. Many commentators have observed that "The bloom is off the rose of the M.B.A." or "The M.B.A. boom is over."

What caused this apparent decline in the value of the M.B.A.? Several factors seemed to have operated together to deflate the value of the degree. First, there is the simple matter of the relationship between supply and demand. Thirty years ago, fewer than 20,000 new M.B.A.s entered the workplace each year. Today, the number is about four times that many. As every student learned in Economics 101, when the supply of a good is great, the price that buyers have to pay for that good will be depressed. Not surprisingly, this fundamental principle of economics applies to the market for M.B.A.s. Given the greater number of graduates, the average price employers are willing to pay for an M.B.A. is lower.

Second, some M.B.A. degrees are, to borrow from George Orwell's *Animal Farm*, "more equal than others." Given that there are several hundred M.B.A. programs, sound common sense dictates that there will be some sort of pecking order. Only a handful of institutions will have a national reputation and the recruiter drawing power that comes with it. Many more will have only regional reputations and correspondingly less job-getting ability for their graduates. And many programs will attract students and employers from a very narrowly circumscribed area. An M.B.A. from certain elite schools is still a trump card; one from a second- or third-tier school may still do the trick; but a degree from many schools may have only very limited and highly specialized utility. In other words, given the increased number of programs, the price that employers are willing to pay for an M.B.A. that is not "top of the line" is lower.

Third, changes in the economic climate and in the way that corporations are organized have affected the value of an M.B.A. During times of economic expansion, the demand for a credential like the M.B.A. is almost certain to be greater than during a period of stability or even contraction. Additionally, the rapid growth in the number of M.B.A.s coincided (whether as cause or effect or both) with a new confidence in the philosophy that "bigger is better." A large conglomerate with diversified holdings is a perfect place for someone trained in abstract concepts of "management" as opposed to someone with concrete experience in a particular business. As companies reorganize and down-size, there will be fewer positions that seem to require that they be filled by someone with an M.B.A.

HISTORICAL PERSPECTIVE

In the 1970s, many people were dissatisfied with their employment prospects and decided to change careers. Schoolteachers, newspaper reporters, historians, artists, homemakers, police officers, and many other people from a wide variety of occupations determined that a professional graduate degree would be just the thing to help guarantee their futures. Most reasoned, "I can't really hope to go to medical school, because I don't have the necessary science background; therefore, I'll go to law school." And the 1970s saw a tremendous surge in applications to law schools. As a consequence, existing law schools expanded enrollments, and new law schools were organized.

By the late 1970s, the common wisdom was that there was a glut of lawyers, but this perception did not deter the career changers. Instead, they reasoned, "I can't really hope to go to medical school because I don't have the necessary science background; and now there is a glut of lawyers; therefore, I'll go to business school." Like the surf, the swell of law school applications crested only to be followed by a swell of business school applications. And since then, the number of schools offering M.B.A. programs has doubled.

Because the late 1970s belonged to the Golden Age of the M.B.A., things turned out well for many of the people who chose business school "by default." In today's economic and business climate, such a decision may not have such serendipitous results. To be sure, some employers may be very attracted to the "three-dimensional" applicant whose life history includes unusual or even offbeat experiences—particularly if that person is graduating from a top-tier school. It is important, however, to understand that other employers may be looking for a proven track record in a position with managerial responsibility. For these employers, the M.B.A. is the wrapping on the package and not the gift itself.

For someone changing careers, the M.B.A. in and of itself is no guarantee of professional advancement. Yet, for many people the M.B.A. still seems to be surrounded by a certain golden aura. It is important to understand, however, that to a certain extent the seeming value of the degree may be a lingering aftermath of a bygone era.

TO B-SCHOOL OR NOT TO B-SCHOOL

If the preceding section seems a bit negative, you should know that the tone was intentional. It was taken in an effort to forestall any unrealistic expectations readers might have about what it means to own an M.B.A.

Now, at this juncture, you would probably expect to see the following advice:

> Determine whether an M.B.A. makes sense for you as an *investment!* Add up the costs of obtaining the degree (including living expenses such as room and board as well as tuition and related costs) and the foregone opportunity costs (including two years of lost salary and benefits). Then assess the benefits of having the degree by calculating the additional earning power that you will have after you graduate.

To be sure, the idea of treating an M.B.A. as an "investment" seems to be appropriate for a book that has the word "business" in its title. (You will find this advice or some variation in many other books and articles on business school admissions.) In reality, however, such advice makes little sense for most people.

Indeed, the advice, at least as written, is so overly simplistic as to fall into outright error. In the first place, why include "living expenses" in the cost of the "investment"? You have to eat during the two academic years anyway, and presumably you will live somewhere. Since those expenses would be incurred in any event, they hardly count as a cost of studying for an M.B.A. Or consider the cost of "two years of lost salary." This point ignores the fact that most M.B.A. students will have summer jobs between their first and second years, and it fails to take account of the fact that most M.B.A.s will begin new jobs immediately after graduation. Thus, the "down time" is actually only eighteen, not twenty-four, months.

Then, how will you project the increase in earning power? The "average starting salary" for the graduates of a business school is just that, an average. How can you project whether you will end up at the top of the class, or at the bottom, or in the middle? What part of the average starting salary of graduates reflects work experience *prior* to entering business school? And what of the graduates of an entrepreneurial bent who decide to go into business for themselves?

Even if it were possible to quantify such variables, there would then be other, nonquantifiable factors to take into account. Some people enjoy the two years of student life; others hate it. Into which category will you fall? How much self-esteem is there to be derived from knowing that you earned an M.B.A.? What will be the likely impact on your family life? Although it is possible to speak of "lost family time" as a "cost" of an investment and of an increase in self-esteem as a "return" on an investment, the analogy seems stretched so thin as to be of little use.

Instead, you will likely make more progress on the question of whether or not an M.B.A. makes sense for you if you address the following questions:

What Do I Expect to Learn from an M.B.A. Program?

The prototypical M.B.A. program is four semesters long. During that time, you will take twenty or so courses, some of them required, while completing any other mandatory workshop, field project, or other specialty programs that might also be part of the curriculum. Even given considerable flexibility, it is almost inevitable that you will find it necessary to take courses in which you have no real interest in order to meet the academic requirements for graduation. This should not, in and of itself, deter you from pursuing the M.B.A. If, however, your needs are extremely narrow, or if your expectations are insufficiently defined, you might want to reconsider your decision to commit the time needed to earn an M.B.A.

If you are considering graduate study in management because your career plans require that you learn more about a particular topic (one that will be only a small part of your two years of study), then you might be better advised to find an alternative to a full-blown M.B.A. program. Perhaps an executive M.B.A. program or a continuing-education program might be the better choice. If you have highly specific expectations about a business school program, then you should review the literature of those schools that you are considering, paying particular attention to the curriculum offerings. If you cannot find at least ten courses that you would put on either a "must have" or a "would gladly take" list, then you may find that fully half of your work toward the M.B.A. is simply irrelevant to your career goals. (Of course, it could turn out that you find that after exposure to a topic in which you had no prior interest, you learn that it is actually your life's passion. But as a rule, taking an M.B.A. in the hopes of finding one's life goal seems a poor gamble.)

It is equally risky to pursue an M.B.A. because you are vaguely dissatisfied with your present career prospects and hope that business school might be a remedy for your malaise. Again, the best advice is to review the curriculum offerings of the schools you are considering. If you cannot put ten or more courses on either a "must take" or "looks great" list, then you may be taking the "default path" to business, a route that is advised against.

What Would an M.B.A. Mean to My Career?

In thinking about this question, make sure that you focus on your individual circumstances. It is not enough to reason generally that "An M.B.A. is likely to earn more money than someone without the degree" or "Many people at the top have M.B.A.s." Instead, try to define specifically the ways in which your career prospects would be furthered by an M.B.A.

For those readers who are already on a business track, the question is how the M.B.A. would accelerate progress along that track or how it would facilitate a shift to some other track. And the question is especially important for those readers who are thinking of a change in careers to a business track. As noted above, many employers are not looking just for an M.B.A. Rather, they are looking for someone who has had considerable management experience and who also happens to have an M.B.A.

How Good a School Am I Likely to Get Into?

Chapter 3 discusses business school rankings and cautions against placing too much emphasis on slight differences in positions in a ranking system. There is not likely to be a great deal of difference between a school that is ranked twenty-fifth and one that is ranked thirtieth. On the other hand, there is almost surely a great deal of difference between the school that is ranked fifth and the one that is ranked fiftieth.

As would be expected, the job prospects for those who graduate from the top-ranked business schools are, as a rule, considerably rosier than for those who graduate from schools ranked near the bottom of the list. It is also true, however, that top-ranked schools are generally more costly to attend than those ranked toward the bottom. This inverse relationship suggests the following: The higher or lower the school is ranked, the more likely it is that the M.B.A. will be a good "investment."

At the one extreme, while an M.B.A. from a top school is very costly, it is also very likely that a graduate will command a salary that will offset the cost of the degree. At the other extreme, while an M.B.A. from a school toward the bottom cannot reasonably expect to receive job offers with top salaries, the cost of getting the degree is relatively low, so any increase in earning power will likely offset the cost of the degree. For schools in the middle, where neither measure is extreme, the decision is the most difficult. As a rule, then, if you are accepted by a top school, then the degree likely makes sense from the standpoint of cost. Or, if you plan to attend a school that charges a very low tuition and otherwise have good reasons for pursuing an M.B.A., then the degree also probably makes sense. For schools in the middle, the "cost-benefit" analysis is problematic.

"G" IS FOR THE GMAT

The letters GMAT stand for the Graduate Management Admission Test, a standardized examination administered several times each year at locations around the world. Most business schools use GMAT scores as one factor in their admissions process. The exact use made of and weight given to the GMAT score varies from school to school, but it can be said that the GMAT score is usually one of the most important factors in an application. The final chapter of this book discusses the GMAT in some detail, providing sample problems and presenting strategies to help you maximize your performance on this important test.

The GMAT is written and administered by the Educational Testing Service (ETS). You can obtain registration materials for the GMAT by writing to:

Graduate Management Admission Test
Educational Testing Service
CN6103
Princeton, New Jersey 08541-6103
Telephone: (609) 771-7330

One question you will have to face fairly early in the application process is what to do about preparing for the GMAT. The test preparation options available to you range from an approach as simple as working the few illustrative questions included in the registration materials for the GMAT to a system as elaborate as a six- to eight-week test preparation course with supplemental private tutoring. The question here is not really whether or not to prepare for the GMAT; it is rather what kind of test preparation to do and how much of it. In an arena as competitive as that of the admissions office of a top school, score differentials of even a few points may very well be critical.

To be sure, admissions officers emphatically deny that admissions decisions are made mechanically by reference to GMAT score differentials and insist with equal vigor that "all relevant factors" are taken into account when making decisions on applications. And doubtless the denials and insistences are well founded. Nonetheless, it is also true that, regardless of the flexibility and fairness of an admissions process, if the GMAT score is given any weight in the decision, then there is a point at which even a small difference in a score can be important.

The preparation options available to you can be divided into two broad categories: the home-study option and the live-instruction option. The home-study option relies on materials that are distributed by the GMAT's sponsor, publications that are available in bookstores, or a combination of these materials. The live-instruction option includes commercial test preparation courses, private tutoring, or a combination of both. The various options can be distinguished along three lines: content, style, and cost.

Content

The first way in which to distinguish various test-preparation options is by their content. In reality, however, there is not as much variation along this line as one might expect. In fact, a comprehensive home-study guide will include substantially all of the same coaching strategies, test-taking tips, and review of substantive concepts that are offered by a commercial test-preparation course or private tutor. And, in a way, this is to be expected: the GMAT is the GMAT.

Style

The second way in which to distinguish the options is by style. Here you will find a very important difference—but one that is primarily a matter of personal taste. Many people prefer the flexibility of the home-study option: there are no scheduled class hours and you can proceed at your own pace, neither held back nor pushed on by classmates. Conversely, many other people prefer the more structured format of a test-preparation program which imposes on them a discipline that they might otherwise have lacked and a classroom setting that stimulates them to think and to learn.

Cost

The third way in which to compare options is cost, and here there are important and quantifiable differences. The cost of the home-study option may be as little as $20, while the cost of a full-blown test-preparation program supplemented by private tutoring can be more than $1,000.

So which route is the best? The answer is that no one way of preparing for the GMAT is uniquely correct. Different approaches will be better for different people. If you are a self-starter for whom cost is an important consideration, then the home-study option seems to be your best bet. If you are a person who needs to have some kind of organization imposed on your life from outside and for whom the cost of a test-preparation course would not be burdensome, then that seems to be the better course.

The best advice is that you at least begin with some home-study materials. You might want to pick up a copy of ARCO's *GMAT SuperCourse* (available at most bookstores) and to order from Educational Testing Service (see address above) the *Official Guide to the GMAT*. After working with these two resources for two or three weeks, give yourself a diagnostic test. Your score on the diagnostic test will give you an idea of where you stand in relation to the goal you have set for yourself for the GMAT. If you are already close, then continued home-study will probably be enough to ensure that you reach that goal. If, however, you find that your performance on the diagnostic test is substantially below the level of performance you need to gain admission to your targeted schools, then you may want to consider enrolling in a test-preparation course or finding a private tutor. The advantage of this approach is that it keeps all options open without incurring any unnecessary expense.

TICK, TOCK . . .WATCH THAT CLOCK

A serious mistake, and one often made by people applying to business school, involves scheduling: underestimating the time needed to complete applications and overestimating the time available. As a consequence, applicants wind up rushing to meet deadlines and are often forced to submit applications before completing them adequately.

Consider the complexity of the process. First, you will probably request literature from several different business schools and spend at least an hour or two per school reading bulletins and other descriptive literature. Next, you should budget at least thirty to forty hours to prepare to take the GMAT. And if you plan to take an in-depth coaching course for the GMAT, you can count on spending thirty to forty hours in a classroom and another forty to sixty hours studying outside of class—and that is a conservative estimate. Then, you should expect to spend another three hours or so per application just on mechanics—filling in blanks, sending out requests for transcripts and letters of recommendation, making copies, and other such activities. Setting aside the mechanical aspects of application forms, there is the difficult and time-consuming task of crafting effective responses to essay prompts that differ from school to school. And after all that you still need to schedule time to visit the schools for interviews.

Once you have finished reading this book, it would be a good idea to sit down and make a list of all the things that you are going to have to do and then to draw up a rough schedule of when different tasks must be finished. The application season runs from late September or early October until late January or early March the following year. (This assumes that everyone will be applying to a prototypical program that begins one fall and ends in the spring two years later; you can adjust these observations to meet any special scheduling demands.) Schools revise their application forms annually, and these forms do not become available until September or October. Thus, you cannot actually begin work on the forms until the fall. You can, however, do some preliminary thinking weeks or even months before then about what sort of answers you will give to various questions, and you can review your resume to make sure that it is complete and up-to-date over the summer.

Additionally, many business schools use a "rolling admissions" process; that is, applications are reviewed and given a disposition in the order in which they are received, even before the official application deadline. Given functionally equivalent qualifications, applicants who apply early stand a better chance of acceptance than those who apply later. Applications received or completed after the recommended dates are usually considered only on a space-available basis. Thus, you want to have your completed applications submitted as early in the admissions season as possible.

Finally, the GMAT is administered four times each year—usually in early fall, late fall, midwinter, and late spring. It's a good idea to register for the spring testing session. That will give you a safety cushion in the event of illness or personal emergency. If you wait until the fall test session and then something happens that prevents you from testing on that date, you could miss your application deadline. Also, taking the GMAT in the spring leaves you time to retake the test if your scores are too low.

If you register to take the test in the spring—about eighteen months before you expect to begin classes—you build in an important safety margin. Remember, further, that your preparation for the GMAT should begin about six to eight weeks before you are scheduled to take the exam.

IN CONCLUSION

The decision to pursue a graduate degree in management—in whatever field and by whatever term that degree may be designated—is not a simple one. Although it does not seem possible to quantify precisely the advantages and disadvantages, you should nonetheless examine in detail what a particular M.B.A. program has to offer and consider carefully what benefit you can hope to derive from it. Given the current economic climate and the changing structure of "business," it is probably not a good idea to choose to study graduate management "by default," just because you don't know what else to do. If you finally decide to pursue a graduate degree in management, then you should make sure you have as many options as possible: Start early, plan carefully, cast your nets widely, and try for every possible competitive edge.

INSIDE THE
ADMISSIONS OFFICE

One of the most vexing aspects of the application process is the uncertainty. As an applicant, you would obviously prefer to know what will happen to your application before you submit it—before you pay the application fee and before you put your ego and other feelings at risk. That, of course, is not possible. Unfortunately for applicants, uncertainty is an inherent part of the application process: Some candidates will be accepted and others will not.

If it is not possible to know what will happen to the application, then the next best thing would be to know exactly how the decision is going to be made. Unfortunately, that too is not likely to happen. Each business school, of course, has a formalized decision-making procedure, but it is rarely described in great detail for outsiders. Instead, the description given in informational bulletins is usually very abstract:

> The committee considers all evidence that suggests academic and professional promise.

> Candidates are evaluated on academic, professional, and personal criteria.

> The committee considers each application on its merits.

These descriptions, typical of those given in business school catalogues, are not particularly helpful. From the point of view of an applicant, the admissions process looks like the proverbial "black box": applications go into the admissions office and disappear from sight; some time later they are discharged, some stamped "Approved," the others stamped "Rejected."

While it may not be possible for you to learn about the mechanics of the decision-making process at any particular school, this book can provide you with general descriptions of some typical decision-making systems. These descriptions are *not* intended to be detailed pictures of the systems currently in use at particular business schools. Rather, they are composite pictures that should give you a pretty good idea of what goes on behind the closed doors of admissions offices.

BEHIND CLOSED DOORS

Every business school has its version of the "black box"—its admissions office. At some schools decisions are made by a director of admissions; at others, they are made by a faculty committee; and at still others, they are made by a committee that includes students. Here are composite descriptions of four different admissions processes.

Metro University Business School

The first school takes its name from its location in a large city. At Metro U., applications are processed by a pair of admissions officers who are not themselves members of the faculty. An admissions committee made up of four faculty members has determined that applications with a GPA or GMAT score below certain minimums pose too great an academic risk to justify acceptance. So, the admissions officers at Metro U. simply sort out for automatic rejection applications with numbers below the minimums established by the admissions committee. All of the remaining applications are then read by the admissions officers, who in turn make a recommendation to the admissions committee to accept, reject, wait-list, or delay action on the application. The admissions committee is the actual locus of authority. It reviews the application in light of the recommendation of the admissions officers and makes a final decision. In most cases, though not all, the committee follows the admissions officers' recommendation.

International Business School

The second school is named for its strong international connections. The International Business School attracts a large percentage of its students from countries other than the United States and is consistently ranked by academic and professional organizations as having a very strong program in international business. At IBS, the admissions decisions are made by a committee of five that includes the dean of admissions, the dean of academic affairs, the dean of students, and two second-year students. Decisions are made by majority vote. One of the striking features of the process used by IBS is the freedom of committee members to use their own idiosyncratic criteria to evaluate applications; that is, the committee does not set standards that members must follow. Still, the committee acts unanimously in a remarkably high percentage of cases. This convergence of opinions suggests that even though the different members might describe their evaluational criteria in different terms, there is substantial, if not conscious, agreement on what factors are important.

Howard Hughes School of Business

The third school is part of a large state university. At Hughes, applications are sorted according to GPA and GMAT score, and the dean of admissions, who is not a member of the faculty, has the authority to make final dispositions on certain applications. The dean has the authority to reject applications with a GPA and/or GMAT score below certain minimums. The dean does not, however, have the authority to accept an application in this group. If the dean thinks that an application with numbers below the established minimums should be accepted, then that application must be referred to the admissions committee. Conversely, the dean also has authority to accept applications with GPAs and GMAT scores above different, higher minimums. The dean, however, cannot summarily reject a "strong" application. If the dean believes that for some reason a strong application should be rejected, he or she must forward that application to the whole committee (with the recommendation to reject it), and the fate of the application is decided by majority vote. Of course, a substantial number of applications fall into the middle area between the two cutoffs. The dean reads these and forwards them to the committee with a recommendation.

Ivy League Business School

The fourth and final business school is a top-ranked school. Although Ivy League Business School isn't actually covered with ivy, it is always included on any list of the top ten business schools in the nation. Because of its substantial reputation, Ivy receives applications that far outnumber the available seats in its next entering class. Some years the ratio is as high as five to one. Consequently, the decision-making system at Ivy is designed to process a large volume of applications efficiently. On the other hand, Ivy prides itself on assembling a student body with extraordinarily diverse qualifications—qualifications that simply cannot be reduced to a GPA, a GMAT score, and a certain number of years of experience.

The solution to this dilemma is a system that sorts applications into two groups, "Very Likely or Very Unlikely" and "Possible." Decisions are made by a committee, but it is obviously not reasonable to expect each member of the committee to read every application. Instead, each application is read by either one or two members of the committee. "Very Likely or Very Unlikely" applications are read by only one member of the committee, who then has the authority either to reject the application or to refer it to the committee as a whole for discussion and vote. Applications in the "Possible" category are read by two members of the committee, each of whom has the same choices as a single reader. Either reader can pass an application on to the committee, and often both do. But if neither reader recommends an application for consideration by the whole committee, then it is rejected.

It is easy to see how this system handles the large volume of applications that arrive at Ivy each year while maximizing the admissions committee's ability to uncover those rough gems that Ivy prides itself on. "Very Likely" or "Very Unlikely" applications need only one reader. A "Very Likely" application will be passed on to the committee as a whole by the single reader unless there is some negative in the application that the reader knows would ultimately disqualify it in the eyes of the members of the whole committee. Conversely, a "Very Unlikely" application will be rejected by the single reader and not passed on to the whole committee unless there is something truly remarkable about the candidate that catches the reader's eye. In this respect, the process is efficient. On the other hand, all "Possible" applications are read by two readers, thereby doubling the chance that a truly unusual candidate with seemingly marginal qualifications will receive consideration by the whole committee.

DIFFERENT DESIGNS, SIMILAR RESULTS

Although there are some interesting differences in the mechanics of the procedures sketched above (and therefore further differences between the actual schools used to create the composites), all four procedures are designed to achieve substantially the same result: an acceptable trade-off between reliability and administrative cost. That the different procedures strike different balances between these competing demands can be more easily seen by imagining more extreme cases.

First, imagine an admissions procedure that is entirely mechanical: applications are arranged according to GMAT scores and GPAs, and only the topmost candidates are accepted. This sort of procedure has the advantage of being cheap to administer, but it runs the risk of missing a lot of otherwise qualified candidates who simply happen to have scores below certain specified minimums and of accepting questionable applicants who just happen to have good numbers. In other words, a purely mechanical admissions procedure sacrifices reliability in favor of cost savings.

Second, imagine an admissions procedure that is designed to maximize reliability. This procedure might not use any quantifiable measures such as GMAT scores and GPA. Instead, the school might actually send a representative from the admissions office to spend a week with each candidate. These representatives observe applicants to see how they "work and play with others." At the end of the week, the observers report back to the admissions office with a detailed report and are debriefed for hours by the admissions committee as a whole. This type of admissions procedure would likely be characterized by very high reliability. Few mistakes would be made, but it would be prohibitively costly to administer.

Each of the four composites sketched above represents a different response to the conflict between the desire for reliability and the need to hold down costs. Metro U., for example, gives up some reliability by automatically excluding applications with numbers that fall below a certain level, but it conserves administrative resources by doing so. The decision-making procedure at Ivy, where every application is read by at least one member of the admissions committee, is more costly to run, but it is designed to produce more reliable decisions.

This analysis does not mean that one procedure is inherently better than another. Rather, it is meant to demonstrate that each is an attempt by an institution to find the most favorable trade-off between conflicting demands. Similarly, there is no suggestion that knowing something about the mechanics of a particular decision-making process will be of much use to you in applying to a particular school. Rather, this exercise is meant to help you better understand the roles that both quantitative factors (such as GPA and the GMAT) and nonquantitative factors (such as your work experience or personal background) play in the admissions process. If you understand how these factors are used, then you will be better able to arrange them in your application to maximize your chances of admission.

QUANTITATIVE FACTORS

The decision-making process of virtually every business school relies, to a greater or lesser extent, on two quantitative factors: GMAT score and GPA. In fact, the scoring scale of the GMAT, which ranges from a minimum of 200 to a maximum of 800, was designed to facilitate comparisons of quantitative factors. Many business schools use a mathematical formula to combine these two quantitative factors to produce an "Index." The Index is a single number that represents a quantitative estimate of a candidate's ability. Here is a formula that combines GPA and GMAT score, giving equal weight to each:

$$\frac{\dfrac{\text{GMAT Score}}{200} + \text{GPA}}{2} = \text{Index}$$

The result of dividing the GMAT score, which ranges from 200 to 800, by 200 is a number between 1 and 4 (inclusive); as you know, most college GPAs fall somewhere in that range as well. The formula then simply averages that result with the GPA. For example, consider an applicant with a GMAT score of 600 and a GPA of 3.4:

$$\frac{\dfrac{600}{200} + 3.4}{2} = \frac{3+3.4}{2} = 3.2$$

This formula produces an Index that is fairly intuitive because the result will have the feel of a grade point average. Thus, the result of 3.2 arrived at above suggests that the applicant is a B+. Or a school might adjust the GPA to put it on the same numerical scale as the GMAT:

$$(200 \times GPA) + GMAT = Index$$

Using this formula, our hypothetical applicant would have the following Index:

$$(200 \times 3.4) + 600 = 1280$$

The second formula generates a number that seems more artificial than the first, but that doesn't really matter so long as the person using the number understands what it means when compared to other such numbers.

You will notice that the Index is calculated using only a cumulative undergraduate GPA. The Index is an attempt to quantify the strength of an application using a single, universal scale. Although a significant minority of applicants will have done graduate work, many more applicants will not have done any graduate work. Yet, excepting a few cases (applicants from foreign countries or from universities with nonstandard grading practices), every applicant will have an undergraduate GPA. So the undergraduate GPA is used in the formula because of its universality. This is not to say, however, that graduate marks play no role in the admissions process. It is possible that an applicant's graduate school record would play a very important role—for good or ill—in the assessment of the application. But graduate marks are not included in the Index.

The GMAT score and GPA have value in that they supply a more or less objective and more or less universal standard by which all applications can be assessed. The precise use to which they are put, however, varies from school to school.

BEYOND THE INDEX

One bit of popular wisdom holds that business schools look only at an applicant's GMAT score and GPA, and they ignore "all that other stuff." To be sure, it may be the case that some schools, most likely those found in the lower levels of any ranking, rely solely upon some mathematical formula for admissions decisions: Applicants with an Index above the cutoff are accepted; those below the cutoff are rejected. It would be surprising to learn, however, that this is the general rule.

On the other hand, some candidates have the mistaken impression that they have a chance at every school regardless of their GMAT score or GPA. They make statements like these: "I know that my GMAT is only in the 25th percentile and my GPA is only a 2.7, but I think that Wharton will accept me because I have been working for the past three years as an assistant manager." This reasoning is incorrect. Although business schools do regard work experience as important, the GMAT score and GPA are nonetheless a very important part of the application. A business school is not simply going to ignore them because you have three, four, five, or even ten years of work experience. Even business schools that advertise that their admissions decisions are "based on a wide variety of factors intended to describe the whole person" will turn you down if your GMAT score or GPA is too low.

It is important to keep in mind these two complementary points:

1. Quantitative factors are important.
2. Quantitative factors are not the whole story.

If you had information about the disposition of applications by a business school according to GMAT score and GPA, you would be able to construct a chart describing the decision-making behavior of the admissions office at that school. A typical table might look like the one on page 23:

The table indicates how many applications a hypothetical business school received with certain GMAT scores and GPAs and how many of those applications were accepted. If you study the table, you will see that the data support two important conclusions.

First, factors other than GPA and GMAT score are important. Some applicants were turned down while other applicants who were seemingly less qualified (in terms of GPA and GMAT score) were accepted. For example, the chart shows that 515 applications were received from candidates with GPAs between 3.25 and 3.49 and GMAT scores between the 81st and 90th percentiles. Only about half of those candidates were accepted, while 267 of them were rejected. Yet the adjacent squares (below, to the left, and diagonally to the lower left) clearly show that some candidates with lower GPA and/or GMAT scores were accepted.

The only feasible explanation for this phenomenon is that this business school looks at factors other than the GPA and GMAT score. "Super numbers" are no guarantee of acceptance, and lower numbers may not be an absolute bar. That's the good news. Now for the bad news.

GMAT Percentile	0–10		11–20		21–30		31–40		41–50		51–60		61–70		71–80		81–90		91–99	
GPA	Apps	Adm	Apps	Adm	Apps	Adm	Apps	Adm	Apps	Adm	Apps	Adm	Apps	Adm	Apps	Adm	Apps	Adm	Apps	Adm
3.75+	3	0	3	0	6	0	8	1	10	1	43	4	39	12	61	42	88	81	89	86
3.50–3.74	2	0	12	0	21	0	24	2	26	1	121	8	127	21	158	76	272	213	213	201
3.25–3.49	9	0	26	0	50	0	48	3	75	2	215	15	215	13	307	84	515	267	369	289
3.00–3.24	19	0	39	0	62	0	68	1	110	5	219	12	127	3	264	21	421	52	315	82
2.75–2.99	25	0	50	0	48	0	51	2	83	1	152	6	80	4	139	7	248	11	186	16
2.50–2.74	24	0	43	0	39	0	39	1	69	1	56	4	26	1	68	5	107	4	77	6
2.25–2.49	36	0	28	0	27	0	20	0	8	0	8	0	12	0	29	0	52	0	24	0
2.00–2.24	12	0	13	0	8	0	6	0	9	0	4	0	8	0	7	0	18	0	11	0
Below 2.00	7	0	6	0	2	0	4	0	2	0	6	0	2	0	1	0	5	0	4	0

*For many years, tables like this were included in The Official Guide to MBA Programs published by the Graduate Management Admissions Council. Unfortunately, they are no longer made available. Still, if you consult an older edition of that work, you will find that the data follow the pattern shown in our hypothetical chart, and there is no reason to believe that the decision-making process now generates significantly different results.

The data in the table also show that this school has some minimum standards for GPA and GMAT score. No candidate was admitted whose GMAT score fell below the 30th percentile, and no candidate was admitted whose GPA was lower than 2.50. And though some candidates were admitted whose GMAT scores were between the 31st percentile and the 70th percentile and whose GPAs were between 2.50 and 3.24, the majority of candidates with numbers in those ranges were rejected.

It is not possible to conclude from the pattern of the chart that there is or is not a formal minimum for GPA or GMAT score. (Some business schools do announce that they have set such minimums.) But if no candidate with numbers below a certain level is accepted by a school, then that school has at least de facto minimums for GPA and GMAT scores. In this case, the candidates who were admitted with strikingly low numbers probably had unique qualifications or were admitted under some special program.

A NEW PERSPECTIVE

Before you continue your reading, take a moment to answer the following question:

> What are the three most important qualities that admissions officers look for in a business school applicant?

1.

2.

3.

When this question is asked at our application workshops, the first person recognized almost invariably answers that "leadership ability" is the most important factor. This answer, while frequently offered, is wrong—as you will soon understand.

In this section, you'll see the admissions process from the perspective of the business schools to which you will be applying. Seeing the issues in this way will help you to decide what to say in your application and how to say it. Imagine that you are the director of admissions of a business school. Each year the school receives three to four times as many applications as there are places available in the next year's entering class. How would you decide which applications to accept and which to turn down?

You must keep in mind that as an admissions officer you have respon-sibilities—to your applicants, to your school, and even to society. Each of these responsibilities will influence the way you make your admis-sions decisions.

First, with regard to your applicants, would you want to admit a student who, in your opinion, simply was not capable of graduating? Obviously not. To admit a candidate who would surely fail would do a disservice to that candidate, who would stand to lose a great deal of money, time, and self-esteem.

The same conclusion is dictated by the interest of the school. Would the faculty be happy with a student who could not keep up? Again, the answer is surely no. From the standpoint of the school's budget, do you think that the dean, who has budgeted for faculty salaries and classroom space, would be happy if a significant number of students flunked out and therefore stopped paying tuition? Again, no. From the standpoint of other students, would they not be better served by being surrounded by bright, articulate, eager-to-learn classmates? Of course. In other words, the entire school would be better off if you admit good students who later become successful in business and contribute to the school's endowment!

Finally, as a director of admissions for an important academic institu-tion, you would also be aware of the influence that your decisions may have on the structure of society. While an M.B.A. is neither a prerequi-site to entering business nor a guarantee of success, it nonetheless can be an important tool for advancement to a position of power. To a certain extent, then, you function as a gatekeeper, and you would want to make sure that those who passed through your doors were morally fit for the roles for which you were preparing them. Furthermore, you would want to give all people an equal opportunity to grab the brass ring that you offer.

ABILITY

Given these concerns, you would probably first read an application to determine whether or not the candidate has the ability to success-fully complete the business school curriculum, which ability—you hope—would also help to make the graduate a success in business. If the application is devoid of any evidence of ability, you would probably reject it—even if the candidate is the child of a large contributor to the school. (Or at least you would try to get the application off your desk and make its disposition the responsibility of someone else—perhaps the dean.)

What constitutes evidence of ability? The past academic record of the applicant, including the GPA, is a readily available measure of past academic ability, but course requirements and standards of grading vary from school to school. The GMAT is designed to give you an objective standard that avoids these difficulties. To be sure, the GMAT is not a perfect testing instrument, and the sponsors of the exam are always at pains to make sure that admissions officers understand the limitations of the test. But admissions officers, as a group, have sufficient confidence in the test that it continues to be an important part of the admissions process.

You can see now that institutional considerations—the importance of finding candidates with the requisite academic ability—would lead an admissions officer to rely heavily on the GPA and the GMAT. This explains the pattern of admissions seen in the table discussed in the preceding section. But other considerations explain the limitation of these factors.

A grade point average is, as the phrase indicates, an average, and an average does not contain certain information about a candidate's ability that you, as an admissions officer, might want to use in making your decision. It would be important to know, for example, whether there was any trend to an applicant's grades. A student's GPA can be pulled down by one or two unrepresentative semesters. Some students require a longer time to adjust to the rigors of college study. Their later grades are likely to be much higher than their first-year marks, but the first-year result will still pull down the overall GPA. As an admissions officer, you might be willing to discount those earlier grades and to rely on the later performance as a better indicator of a candidate's ability. And you would certainly want to discount a single unrepresentative semester, particularly if the candidate can explain that circumstances such as personal illness or a death in the family interfered with studying that semester.

You would also want to look closely at a candidate's transcript to assess the quality of work that was needed to generate the GPA. As you examine the transcript, you would try to determine whether the mix of courses taken was academically challenging and whether there were any especially difficult courses. It would also be a good idea to learn something about the life experiences that surrounded the candidate's undergraduate study. Factors such as part-time work or family responsibilities would be important in interpreting what the GPA means in terms of ability.

You would also want to place some weight on the candidate's graduate studies, if any. To the extent that the graduate marks either support or contradict the conclusion suggested by the undergraduate GPA, this information could be important. If a candidate with a relatively low undergraduate GPA returned to school as a more mature person and did very well, you would probably conclude that the later performance at the graduate level is better evidence of that person's ability than the earlier undergraduate marks.

A second major indicator of a candidate's ability would be professional accomplishments, and your starting point here might be a listing of employers, positions, and dates on the application form. This type of listing, however, suffers from the same defect that we found in the GPA: it is much too general. For example, the title "vice president" doesn't say very much about the applicant's responsibilities or accomplishments. Consequently, you would probably invite applicants to submit their resumés and even give them an opportunity to explain the significance of their professional accomplishments in greater detail in writing or in a personal interview.

As you review an applicant's employment history in your search for evidence of ability, you would be looking for the answers to two questions. First, was the applicant given the opportunity to exercise meaningful managerial responsibilities? Second, did the applicant successfully discharge those responsibilities?

Other aspects of an applicant's background might also suggest the presence of ability. A position of leadership in an extracurricular activity while in college or in a civic organization after graduation might be evidence of an ability to direct other people, organize tasks, or communicate effectively. The significance of the accomplishment and the weight to be given it would obviously depend upon particular details.

The point is that you, as director of admissions, would want to be satisfied—for the sake of the applicant and for the sake of the school—that the applicant has the "raw intellectual horsepower" to get the job done. Consequently, you are not looking at previous academic performance, employment experience, and additional activities as past accomplishments. Rather, you are interested in them for what they portend.

MOTIVATION

Let us assume that you are persuaded that an applicant has great ability. Would that be the end of your inquiry? Surely not. Ability alone is not sufficient; there must also be a commitment to put that ability to use. Thus, you would probably not be comfortable accepting a candidate, even one with top numbers, who said, "I don't really want to go to business school, but I thought I might try it for a while to see whether I like it."

What kind of evidence might there be of commitment or motivation? In general, past academic success is strongly suggestive of commitment and motivation, because past success demonstrates that the applicant can set goals and then attain them. The same can be said of professional success, for a strong resumé indicates that a candidate has the "stick-to-it-iveness" required for both academic study and long-term career development. Finally, participation in extracurricular activities or community service could also be evidence of a sense of maturity and responsibility. Again, it should be emphasized that you, as an admissions officer, would not just be tallying up past accomplishments. You would be searching for evidence that an applicant has shown commitment to past undertakings and so will likely have a similar sense of commitment to future activities.

SOMETHING EXTRA

Thus far, you have decided that a successful applicant should show strong evidence of both ability and commitment. Ability without commitment is just raw energy without direction and is doomed to failure. But without ability, commitment, no matter how sincerely and strongly felt, is impotent. Both qualities are necessary.

Now suppose that you receive 1,000 applications for the 250 places in next year's entering class. And after eliminating those who lack either ability or motivation or both, you are still left with 550 applications. A few of those stand out as superstars, and you will of course want to accept them. But you still have about twice as many applications as you can accept—even though you have satisfied yourself that all of them can successfully do the academic work of your M.B.A. program and will likely go on to successful careers in whatever they do. You could fill the remaining seats just by taking those with the very best GMAT scores and GPAs; while that strategy might boost your school's "median class score," it lacks imagination.

Suppose that you have a choice between two applicants with very close numbers, comparable performances in college, and similar professional careers. One of the applicants, however, is an amateur musician who plays the violin in the community orchestra. The other has no comparable achievement. Which candidate would you prefer? Remember, admissions officers are also looking to put together an interesting group of people who will bring with them different talents and perspectives.

In other words, if all other considerations are equal, you would opt for a candidate who is able to bring an additional dimension to the student body. This additional dimension could be expressed in many different ways: athletic ability, unusual family background, artistic talent, significant travel experience, and so on. Anything that an individual might contribute could conceivably catch your eye and become that "little bit extra" that prompts you to recommend that application over another.

DIVERSITY

Finally, your institution probably also has a commitment to ensuring that its student body is reflective of the diversity of society, and to that end you may be charged with implementing measures designed to guarantee that members of various groups are included in each entering class. Does this mean that, for certain groups of applicants, you will simply abandon the search for ability and commitment? Not at all. Rather, your treatment of these applications is just a logical extension of your other procedures. Just as you realize that a GPA can be better understood in light of the particular experiences of an applicant as an undergraduate, so too you reason that family history and social background can also be used to interpret past accomplishments. For example, a 3.5 GPA earned by the first person in a family to attend college may be viewed as a greater accomplishment than a 3.5 GPA earned by a student who comes from a family where both parents are college graduates.

Additionally, you may have reason to believe that the GMAT doesn't have the same validity for all groups in the applicant pool. If, for example, based on records of students who have attended your institution, you have determined that the GMAT underpredicts the performance of a certain group of candidates, you would adjust your thinking about the GMAT scores of those candidates. You wouldn't change your goal of finding qualified and motivated students, but you would interpret the evidence provided by the GMAT differently. The GMAT is in a sense defective when applied to these candidates.

IN CONCLUSION

As you can see, an admissions process that strives for reliability—that is, one that strives to select an entering class of highly qualified and motivated individuals who bring with them unique experiences and who embody considerable diversity—is enormously complex. Such a process necessarily goes beyond a purely mechanical rank ordering of Indexes generated by a mathematical formula using only GPAs and GMAT scores. And you should now understand why business schools ask for supporting documentation such as personal statements and letters of recommendation and why they want you to visit for a personal interview, if possible.

The subsequent chapters in this book will discuss strategies for making the most of these additional opportunities for influencing admissions officers and committees.

TARGETING SCHOOLS

Business-school applicants tend to be a heterogeneous group. They come from different social and cultural backgrounds, have different educational and professional experiences, and have different career goals. These differences make any discussion of targeting schools somewhat problematic.

On the one hand, there are some applicants whose business-school options are limited by very particular circumstances. Family ties may require that a person remain in a certain area, or professional responsibilities may mean that a part-time program is the only viable option. Similarly, financial constraints may dictate that only public institutions can be considered. For those who find themselves in such circumstances, the number of options may be so limited that it doesn't really make sense to worry about "targeting" schools, the subject of this chapter. If you fall into this group, then you will quickly realize that this chapter isn't particularly important to you. (You may, however, find some of the information interesting, particularly the discussion of business school rankings.)

On the other hand, many applicants want to get into the best school possible and are willing to relocate to accomplish this. If you fall into this category, then there are literally hundreds of schools that you might consider. And even if you limit yourself to a specific geographic region, you will still have dozens of options. Therefore, it is necessary to find some way to reduce the number of possibilities to a manageable group. That task is the focus of this chapter.

REPUTATION AND NAME RECOGNITION

As noted, many people are willing to cast their application nets fairly wide, hoping to enroll at the "best" school they possibly can. This strategy can be described by the dictum "Apply to the best, and hope for the best." Of course, it's a strategy that can't be used by everyone, because not everyone will have a realistic chance of being accepted by a top school. And because the competition at the best schools is keen, even those with exceptional qualifications cannot be guaranteed acceptance. Thus, the strategy might better be described as "Apply to the best school you can reasonably expect to get into, and hope for the best result." This strategy makes a lot of sense for people who are not operating under any personal, professional, or financial constraint.

Since this strategy advises candidates to apply to the best schools that are within reach, it obviously requires some way of comparing schools and determining which are better than others. Candidates usually interpret this requirement to mean that they should find some way of learning about the "reputation" of each school that they might be considering. While the instinct to inquire after reputation is understandable, the attempt to compare business schools on the basis of their reputations must ultimately end unsatisfactorily, for several reasons.

In the first place, reputation, which is public opinion, must be distinguished from reality; opinion obviously does not equal fact. It doesn't take too much effort, for example, to recollect personal acquaintances whose reputations, either for good or for ill, simply did not accurately reflect their true characters. Surely a good part of the disparity between reputation and fact can be explained by lack of information. It's impossible to know everyone with the same degree of familiarity. A similar phenomenon characterizes opinions about business schools.

First, very few people are sufficiently familiar with several different business schools to offer an enlightened opinion about the strengths and weaknesses of the programs offered by each. After all, what reason would someone have for being so knowledgeable about the workings of a dozen or so different business schools? To be sure, an academic type such as a dean might have such information—but could hardly be expected to share it with prospective applicants. An experienced corporate recruiter might also have insight into different business schools, but that person's time is so valuable that it would be unreasonable to hope to get the information. Thus, a search for information about business school reputations would probably force us to ask for the opinions of people who aren't in the best position to form such opinions.

Second, educational institutions are not immune from the economic forces that shape markets. Demand and luck help determine whether a business school is successful, and as conditions change so too will the effectiveness of schools change. Public opinion, however, usually lags behind these changes by several years. Consequently, a business school's reputation may be a shared opinion that is badly out of date. A well-established school that allows the educational quality of its programs to deteriorate will nonetheless continue to enjoy its earlier reputation for some time. Conversely, a younger school that through vision and aggressive administration makes substantial improvements in the quality of its programs in just a few years may still have a reputation as a somewhat immature institution, even though that judgment is no longer accurate.

The third and most important reason why the attempt to compare schools according to reputation must fail is revealed by the following question: Is reputation a difference that makes a difference? Consider the following scenario about a school that will be called the Nomen Magnus Business School. Nomen Magnus enjoys a reputation as the very best business school in the country. When business professionals or academics are asked to name the best business school, they invariably respond, "Why, Nomen Magnus—of course!" Yet the graduates of Nomen Magnus just cannot seem to find jobs. When asked about this seeming disparity, the so-called experts respond, "Yes, we all know that its students do not get hired, but we still consider Nomen Magnus to be the best."

What is wrong with this picture? It's obviously completely illogical. After all, one means of determining that one business school is better than another is to establish that it provides its graduates with better job prospects than the other school. Even though placement is not the only criterion that can be used to judge a business school, the thought experiment of the preceding paragraph makes the point that the abstract notion of reputation isn't really a reliable basis for comparing business schools.

If business schools cannot be compared according to their reputations, then how can they be compared? The scenario described above has already hinted that the abstract notion of reputation is actually shorthand for a cluster of more concrete—and quantifiable—considerations, such as placement record. Therefore, rather than worrying about reputation, let's concentrate on the specific measures that together help to create the public perception of a school's general effectiveness.

PUBLISHED RANKINGS

Several publications offer rankings of business schools that you might find useful. One of the most popular is the "Annual Survey" published by *U.S. News and World Report* each spring. In addition to a rank-ordered list of the top business schools, the article usually includes an overview of trends in graduate management education as well as two or three box inserts featuring up-and-coming schools or schools that offer a particular concentration. *Business Week* has published a book-length guide to *The Best Business Schools*. It includes in-depth profiles of the top forty business schools in the United States as well as a ranking system that orders the top twenty business schools. *The Insider's Guide to the Top Ten Business Schools* offers over 300 pages of descriptive material about top business schools, but does not provide its own ranking system. Rather, the editor chose to rely on already published rankings to choose the top ten. Also, ARCO publishes a book entitled *The Best Graduate Business Schools*, which offers profiles of the top twenty-five schools plus fifteen runners-up. You can use any of these references with a fair degree of confidence—provided that you keep in mind the following points.

Rankings tend to be controversial—at least for the schools that are the subject of the ranking. In fact, only one school (the one with the top ranking) is likely to be completely satisfied by a particular result. In this regard, the Graduate Management Admission Council (GMAC)—a quasi-official association of business schools—offers the following advice about any ranking of business schools:

> The ranking of all kinds of educational programs has become one of the most popular of American indoor sports, and this is especially so for M.B.A. programs. While it is certainly valuable to have a comparative view of the programs of different schools, you should also remember that any ranking is, at best, a short-hand method of evaluating educational quality. The methodology used in any particular ranking will affect its outcome, and these methodologies are not always made clear. Further, such rankings do not adequately address the tremendous variety that characterizes graduate management education today. Given the differences between schools, ranking schemes that attempt to enforce uniformity often end up comparing apples and oranges. A heavy reliance on such rankings can do you a great disservice

as an applicant, for it may lead to an unnecessary narrowing of your choices. Choosing the right M.B.A. program is a task that requires real effort in collecting information, evaluating your personal goals, and thinking realistically about your choices. You owe it to yourself to do this, and not simply to follow the advice of some anonymous "expert."*

This advisory makes two very good points. In the first place, a ranking system necessarily employs a methodology. Most often, a ranking system will identify certain factors that are deemed to be good measures of a business school's effectiveness and solicit relevant data from schools themselves by means of a survey. The data are then combined using a formula to produce the ranking system.

You need to pay careful attention to the methodology used to create a ranking system—not because you should expect to find any sleight-of-hand or outright errors, but because you will want to make sure that the factors used to create the ranking are factors that are important to you. For example, one ranking system incorporates satisfaction with school-provided student housing. Although this is a relatively minor factor in the overall ranking, someone for whom school-provided housing is not an issue might want to adjust, at least informally, the final result by deleting this factor.

If a ranking is not accompanied by an explanation of the methodology used to produce the ranking, then you should regard it with some suspicion. For example, one of the publications mentioned above does not offer an independent ranking but relies instead upon "recent ratings." Obviously, then, the fact that a business school is included in that publication is not *independent* evidence that it is a top school. In other words, that publication does not really provide a new ranking.

Second, as the GMAC notes, a ranking system necessarily imposes uniformity upon a complex situation. In order to achieve this uniformity, the system must abstract from all particular content. After all, the very purpose of the mathematical formula is to reduce everything to a single number, but there is a price that must be paid for this abstraction. Take something as seemingly unproblematic as "average starting salary of graduates." Surely, "average starting salary" is just about as pure a measure as one could ever hope to find for a business school's job-getting ability. Yet, "average starting salary," as a single number, does not take

---

Graduate Management Admission Council, The Official Guide to MBA Programs (Princeton, N.J.: Graduate Management Admission Council, 1992), 20.

account of the fact that the starting salaries of graduates may depend to a significant degree on the extent of their professional experience *prior* to entering business school. Nor does "average starting salary" say anything about the types of jobs in which the graduates were placed nor the fields into which they went.

It is important, then, not to place too much reliance on a ranking. While it is useful to have some idea of how one school matches up against another, there are too many variables that simply cannot be captured by a single formula. You would indeed do yourself a disservice if you refused to consider a particular school simply because it did not have a certain position in a ranking.

Beyond the two points made by the GMAC, there is a further important consideration to keep in mind when using a ranking. Since a ranking system uses a linear order, it gives the impression of great precision: since one is less than two and five less than six, the school ranked number one must be significantly better than the school ranked number two, and the school ranked number five must be significantly better than the school ranked number six. Fortunately, most applicants are too sophisticated to make such a simplistic error. When two schools are very close in a ranking, say only one position apart, it would be a mistake to conclude that one is clearly better than the other.

Most people, however, would likely defend the proposition that since one is much less than six, the school ranked number one must surely be better than the school ranked number six. Consequently, if Harvard Business School is ranked number one and Sloan is ranked number six, then it must surely follow that Harvard really is better than Sloan. Despite its persuasive appeal, this logic is flawed. Consider the following remark included in a recent *U.S. News and World Report* survey of business schools:

> Stanford edged out Harvard—which had finished as the No. 1 school [last year]—to win top honors in this year's survey of M.B.A. programs. Harvard fell to third place, while its Cambridge neighbor, the Sloan School at the Massachusetts Institute of Technology, jumped from sixth to second.

In other words:

Last Year	This Year
1. Harvard	1. ——
2. ——	2. Sloan
3. ——	3. Harvard
4. ——	4. ——
5. ——	5. ——
6. Sloan	6. ——

It is difficult to imagine what sort of change in the objective conditions at Harvard and Sloan could account for this result: last year Harvard was clearly better than Sloan, but this year Sloan is marginally better than Harvard.

Of course, a closer look at the data would turn up an explanation for the seemingly anomalous result. Perhaps, for example, this year's survey of deans just happened to include individuals who think that the academic reputations of the two schools are very close. Perhaps a larger portion of Sloan's graduates responded to the placement office's employment survey, and this increase in reporting raised Sloan's position on the "average starting salary" scale. Which of the two years, last year or this year, provides the more accurate picture? The answer is neither.

Unless it can be established that one or the other survey contained an error, then there is no reason to prefer one over the other. Of course, if the two surveys were separated by a period of ten years, then there would be reason to prefer the more recent one. But there is absolutely no reason to believe that in just twelve months Harvard screwed up so badly and the Sloan School made such mind-boggling improvements that their order really should be reversed. Rather, the conclusion to be drawn is that, in a ranking such as this one, the number-one school and the number-six school are probably not really very far apart in terms of quality.

Although a ranking system usually presents its results in a linear order, you should not feel constrained by its linearity. Rather, you should think in terms of ranges. Thus, if Harvard is ranked number one, then you might treat its "true rank" as being somewhere between one and six, and if the Sloan School is ranked number six, you might treat its "true rank" as being somewhere between one and eleven. If you think in ranges, you will see that there is truly some wisdom in the old adage "There are fifteen schools in the top ten."

A ranking can also be misleading in yet another way. When a ranking includes only the top n schools, the school with the ranking $n + 1$ is not included in the list. The ranking necessarily creates a distinction between 1 through n and all other schools, and no further distinction is made among all other schools. They are simply the ones not included in the list. Because a reader has no way of knowing which school in the group of those not included has the $n + 1$ rank, the ranking creates the misleading impression that all of those not included on the list are pretty much the same; that is, $n + 1$ is pretty much equal to $n + 101$. And although we might not want to draw too fine a distinction based upon a ranking (as discussed above), we would not want to say schools cannot be ranked quantitatively.

Some surveys try to mitigate the severity of this problem by including an alphabetized list of "also-rans." Such a list is useful because it lets the reader know which other schools might have been included in the list of top schools, but there remains a third group not included either in the top schools or the also-rans. You have to keep in mind that some schools in this third group were very close to qualifying for the also-ran list.

CREATING YOUR OWN RANKINGS

Some published rankings also suffer from the further limitation that they include only a small percentage of the total number of accredited business schools. (The *Official Guide to MBA Programs* that is prepared by the GMAC has approximately 600 entries.) How is it possible to compare programs that are not included in one or another published ranking? The answer is to create your own rankings.

Of course, you will not need to include in your rankings every business school not already covered by a published ranking—only those in which you have an interest. (You may also want to include some of those covered in published rankings to see how they would rank under your system.) Additionally, your system will probably not be quite as sophisticated as that used by a large publisher. You probably would not, for example, consider mailing out extensive survey questionnaires to all of the Fortune 500 companies asking their CEOs to give opinions about graduates from various business schools. (And you probably wouldn't get very many answers if you did.)

A fairly primitive, but fairly effective, ranking system can be created using the average (or median) GPA and GMAT score of each school's most recent entering class. You can combine those two numbers using the following formula:

$$\text{Index} = \frac{(\text{GMAT} \div 200) + \text{GPA}}{2}$$

The effect of the formula is to weight equally the average GMAT score and the average GPA for each school to create a single number that has the "feel" of a Grade Point Average. Let us take some hypothetical numbers:

School	Average GPA	Average GMAT
Alpha	3.3	580
Beta	3.1	500
Gamma	3.6	700
Delta	3.4	620
Epsilon	3.0	460

The ranking of these five schools would be:

1. Gamma   (3.55)
2. Delta   (3.25)
3. Alpha   (3.10)
4. Beta   (2.80)
5. Epsilon (2.65)

All of the caveats explained above regarding rankings apply to any ranking generated in this way, and with even greater force because of the primitiveness of the system.

You can, if you choose, create a more elaborate system by increasing the number of variables used in creating the ranking. You might, for example, include information about the school's placement record. The average (or median) starting salary of last year's graduating class and the percentage of the class who had positions at graduation would give you rough measures of a school's "placement power." And a school's faculty-to-student ratio and the total number of volumes in its library might serve as rough measures of the school's educational resources. It might even be fun to use a spreadsheet program to play around with these and other variables to see what patterns emerged. Ultimately, however, any impression of precision beyond that conveyed by the simpler two-factor system using average GPA and average GMAT score is likely to be an illusion.

Furthermore, as the differences between schools become increasingly difficult to quantify, their importance is more likely to be outweighed by qualitative differences. So instead of trying to create a more refined quantitative analysis to separate schools, you would be better advised to start concentrating on other factors, such as geographical location and cost.

THE TOP BUSINESS SCHOOLS

What are the top business schools? Given what we know about business-school education and what we have learned from published rankings and other sources, we would answer that some mix of the following ten schools (listed in alphabetical order) should make up the list of the top five schools:

> University of Chicago
>
> Columbia University
>
> Dartmouth College (Amos Tuck)
>
> Harvard University
>
> Massachusetts Institute of Technology (Sloan)
>
> University of Michigan
>
> Northwestern University (Kellogg)
>
> University of Pennsylvania (Wharton)
>
> Stanford University
>
> Yale University

Then, five of the following ten schools (listed in alphabetical order) should be combined with the five schools above that were not included in the list of the top five schools to make up the list of schools ranked six through fifteen:

> Carnegie-Mellon University
>
> Cornell University (Johnson)
>
> University of California at Berkeley (Haas)
>
> University of California at Hastings
>
> University of California at Los Angeles (Anderson)
>
> Duke University (Fuqua)

Georgetown University

New York University (Stern)

University of Texas at Austin

University of Virginia (Darden)

Then the five left over from the list above should be grouped with five schools from yet another group of ten schools to make up the list of schools ranked sixteen through twenty-five—and so on.

CAVEAT EMPTOR

An important source of information about a business school is its bulletin. There, you will usually find a listing of course offerings, a description of special features such as foreign-exchange programs and internships, brief faculty biographies, and a summary of some of the accomplishments of various members of the student body.

Although business school bulletins are an important source of information, it is necessary to keep in mind who prepared them. A school's bulletin was written to attract "customers," and you can bet that it was carefully prepared to present the school in the best possible light— including laudatory quotations from recent graduates and color photographs of smiling students. A bulletin is likely to highlight the most interesting courses offered at the school and is not likely to mention those that current students know are as "dull as dry toast." When describing faculty, a bulletin will feature the school's "big guns" but not mention that many courses are taught by adjunct or part-time faculty. As for those business schools that are part of large universities, their bulletins typically incorporate by reference the resources and facilities of the university as a whole, such as "Central Library with 1,000,000 volumes" but do not point out that few if any of those books are ever actually used by business school students.

Additionally, bulletins make liberal use of all the current buzzwords. Thus, you are likely to find statements such as:

We are seeing the inevitable emergence of a global community. National boundaries are becoming increasingly irrelevant to commerce and finance. The international dimension of our program is designed to equip managers of the twenty-first century to face these new challenges.

> The key to effective management in the future will be multidi-
> mensional thinking. Our highly acclaimed interdisciplinary
> approach brings together professionals from a variety of fields
> who are able to cross-fertilize one another's thinking.

And what does all of this mean? Who knows!

As noted in chapter 1, no consensus exists about exactly what it is that business schools can, do, or should accomplish. This is not to say that claims of the sort set out above are meaningless; it is rather to say that their meanings are not completely clear. The best advice is that you should visit as many schools as possible to find out how current students feel about the various "high-tech" features of the curriculum. And then there is always the bottom line: Do employers, who are the ultimate "consumers" of M.B.A.s, buy this theory? That question is answered by the track record of the school's placement office.

CREATING A SHORT LIST

At some point, perhaps after considering many schools, you will need to sit down and make a "short list"—a list of the schools that you will actually apply to. Many prospective applicants ask, "Which schools should I apply to?" The answer to that question is another question: "How many do you plan to apply to?" And for the question, "How many schools should I apply to?" the response is, "Which would you like to apply to?" There is an obvious circularity here, but it's one that cannot be avoided because it is impossible to answer one of the questions independently of the other.

In one respect, an answer to the "how many" question depends on an answer to the "where" question. For a very strong candidate who plans to focus on a few top schools, the answer is "just a few." For a candidate with above-average but not outstanding qualifications who wants to get into a top school, the answer is "many." For a candidate with average qualifications who wants to attend a particular local school for which average qualifications are more than acceptable, the answer is just that one school (plus an insurance school, or perhaps two). For a candidate with marginal qualifications who really wants to go to business school, the answer is "as many as you can afford."

On the other hand, an answer to the "where" question may also depend upon an answer to the "how many" question. A candidate with only limited resources who plans to submit only two or three applications must be very conservative and apply to schools at which the chances for acceptance are very, very good. But a candidate with unlimited resources who can afford to apply to dozens of schools, including some for which the chances for acceptance are fairly slim, can afford to apply to long shots as well as sure things.

For most people, finalizing a list of business schools to apply to requires some trade-offs. On the one hand, candidates do want to get into the best school they can. On the other hand, no one would think of applying to every single business school in existence. So you have to balance both competing considerations: In light of what you are able to spend, what mix of schools maximizes your chances of getting into the best possible school while still ensuring that you will be accepted by some schools?

If you apply to only four or five schools, you won't have very much flexibility in creating your short list of target schools. The best advice is to target schools on the assumption that you will apply to ten schools. Study the information provided in the various guides already mentioned and come up with a tentative list of ten schools. At that point, if you feel that there are other schools you want to include (and you can afford the application fees), then expand the list. If you can't afford to apply to ten (or simply don't care to), then decide which schools on the list are most appealing and pare down the list accordingly.

Ultimately, your list of target schools should contain a mix of schools:

■ a couple of "long-shot" or "reach" schools

■ a couple of "sure-thing" or "insurance" schools

■ several "bread-and-butter" or "very likely" schools

Long-shot or reach schools are schools for which your chances are not very good—perhaps only one out of five or even one out of ten—but which have very good programs. A sure-thing or insurance school is a school for which you are almost overqualified, and your chances for acceptance are 80 percent or better. And bread-and-butter or very likely schools are those at which your numbers match, more or less, the average numbers of the most recent entering class.

The three categories of schools must be interpreted in light of your GPA and GMAT score. At the very top, for a candidate with a perfect GMAT score and a 4.0 GPA, there are no reach schools. Assuming that such a candidate has the necessary work experience, even the top schools are this candidate's bread and butter. Nonetheless, even this candidate should apply to some safety schools. For a candidate with less competitive numbers, say a 2.6 GPA and a GMAT score in the thirtieth percentile, there may very well be no safety schools. Schools that many people would consider their bread-and-butter schools are this candidate's reach schools, and this candidate may have to work to get admitted at even one or two schools.

Remember that GPAs and GMAT scores are not the only factors considered by admissions officers. The "unquantifiables" are also very important. The fact is, however, that the quantitative factors may be used to screen applications, and if the quantitative measures are too low the unquantifiables may never even come to light.

As you work on your short list of target schools, it will be necessary for you to try to anticipate how your unquantifiables will be weighed. Unfortunately, it is impossible to predict exactly how the description of your personal experiences will affect a given admissions officer. Our best advice on this count is: Be realistic!

When we do admissions workshops and seminars, we ask for a show of hands from those in attendance to indicate how many have significant work experience and extracurricular activities. Here is what usually happens:

We say, "Everyone who has ever had a full-time or a part-time job, please raise your hand." Every hand goes up.

"Now, everyone who has ever had two such jobs, keep your hands up. Everyone else, put your hand down." Almost every hand stays up.

"Next, everyone who considers that this work experience is not very significant, lower your hand." Virtually no hands go down.

"Everyone please put your hands down, and then everyone with at least one significant extracurricular or community activity, raise your hand again." Virtually everyone raises a hand.

"Everyone with two or more significant extracurricular or community activities, keep your hands up. The rest of you can lower yours." Very few hands are lowered.

"And the same for people with three or more significant activities." Most people still have a hand raised.

This little routine, repeated many times over the years, suggests that most people applying to business school have significant work experience and have participated in important extracurricular or community activities. The intention of this story is not to discourage you from setting your sights high but to caution you that you are likely to find yourself competing against other very-well-qualified candidates.

IN CONCLUSION

Choosing a business school is not an exact science—despite the seeming precision of various ranking systems. Unless you are operating within some special constraints, you should cast your net wide. Do not begin the process with preconceived notions about which schools are better than others or which school might be best for you. Create your personal short list using the three-pronged approach described above.

If you are fortunate enough to receive several acceptances, here's what you should do. Before the deadline for making a decision and paying a tuition deposit, schedule visits to each school that you are considering. The admissions office will arrange for you to sit in on a class or two and take a tour of the facilities. You will also have the opportunity to chat with some students who are already enrolled there and therefore know full well what you can expect.

Finally, you should realize that during the two years you are in school the focus of your life is likely to be the school. Surely this will be true if you take advantage of school housing arrangements; but even if you have a spouse and children, you are likely to find that many of your social contacts are with other business school students with families. Additionally, many of the hours that you may have spent as an undergraduate in the college's rathskeller or coffeehouse will likely be spent in the library's cellar or at home studying. In other words, for two years you will be wed to that school and its students. Make sure in advance that it will be a viable marriage.

ANATOMY OF AN
APPLICATION

This chapter will discuss the various parts of the typical business-school application and methods for ensuring that your application, when completed, will be as effective as possible. Of course, each business school designs its own application forms, so it will be necessary to create a somewhat different application package for each school to which you apply. Additionally, procedures vary from school to school. For example, some schools want transcripts mailed directly to their admissions office, while others want you to include official copies in sealed envelopes along with the rest of your application materials. Still, it is useful to think of the idiosyncrasies of the individual application forms as just so many variations on a main theme, and it is to this main theme that this chapter is devoted. It is important for you to remember, however, that you must follow carefully the exact procedures set forth by each particular school.

For most schools, a completed application must include the following:

Official transcripts

Application fee

Test score(s)

Completed personal data forms

Resumé

Letters of recommendation

Personal interview (not all schools)

Personal statement(s)

You are responsible for initiating the application process and for ensuring that the various elements of the application package arrive at the right admissions office on time. To obtain an application package and descriptive literature, write or telephone the admissions offices at the schools you are interested in. (Note: The personal statement will be addressed in chapter 5.)

TIMING

A business-school application consists of several components. Each component requires several successive steps such as requesting information and completing forms. Some important procedures such as the issuing of official transcripts and the writing of letters of recommendation must be executed by other people and can take several weeks to be completed. Failure to take a key step at the appropriate time can slow down the entire project or even fatally delay completion of the application. Successful orchestration of the various sections of the application requires advance planning and careful attention to detail.

The prototypical business school program involves two consecutive academic years of study. A school that follows this traditional model admits students in the fall or early winter for the next fall semester. Many schools now offer variations on this theme with programs such as mid-year admissions or summer terms. The directions that follow assume that all readers are applying to a traditional program. If you are applying to a business school that offers different options, you should be able to adapt the general comments to the particular requirements of those different options.

Traditionally, a business school begins to accept applications for its next entering class in October—almost a full year before students in that class begin their studies. For schools that still observe this sort of schedule, deadlines for filing applications may come as early as March of the year in which the applicant expects to enroll, though some schools may continue to accept applications into the summer. We refer to this period as an "application season."

Just as the length of its application season is set by each school, the timing of decisions and notifications varies from school to school. In the past, schools accumulated applications until the deadline for accepting applications had passed. Then all applications were reviewed together, decisions were made, and notifications sent. Today, many business schools use a "rolling" admissions process for making decisions. A business school that operates on the rolling-admissions principle reviews applications from time to time throughout the application season. Based on a school's experience with applications in previous years, its admissions officers make projections about the next entering class in terms of GMAT scores, GPAs, and so forth. As soon as a significant number of applications have been received, and in light of the projections, the review process begins.

If you are thinking of applying to a business school that uses a rolling-admissions procedure, you should apply as early in the season as possible, for two reasons. First, you will be notified of the disposition of your application early in the season. Having this information will enable you to make plans for the transition from the workplace or college to graduate study in management. Second, the rolling-admissions process gives a competitive advantage to those who apply earlier. By the time the application season is drawing to a close, relatively few places in the entering class will remain to be allocated. In order to have every possible edge, you should apply early.

Again, remember that different schools have application seasons with different opening and closing dates. Pay careful attention to the descriptive information provided with each application and make certain to complete each one in a timely fashion.

TEST SCORES

To arrange to take the GMAT, you will need to contact:

> Graduate Management Admission Test
> Educational Testing Service
> CN6103
> Princeton, New Jersey 08541-6103
> Telephone: (609) 771-7330

Educational Testing Service (ETS) will forward your test scores directly to the schools that you designate to receive your scores when you register for the GMAT.

If English is not your native language, you will probably also have to take the Test of English as a Foreign Language (TOEFL). To register for that examination, contact:

)EFL
lucational Testing Service
CN2896
Princeton, New Jersey 08541-2896
Telephone: (609) 882-6601

ETS will also forward these test scores directly to the schools that you designate to receive them when you register for the TOEFL.

The GMAT is administered four times each year. The exact dates vary from year to year, but test administrations are usually scheduled in early fall, late fall, midwinter, and late spring. Regular registration for the GMAT closes approximately five weeks before each test date. Late registration closes about two weeks before each test date. (Late registration requires payment of an additional fee.) Score reports become available about six weeks after each test administration.

It is recommended that you take the GMAT *before* the start of the application season in which you plan to participate. Since the test is administered in the winter (usually January or February), the late spring (usually June), and the early autumn (usually October), the best advice is to take the exam in the winter or spring—about eighteen months prior to the time that you plan to start business school.

With a GMAT score already "in the bank," you can use the summer to make some preliminary decisions about what schools you might be interested in and to begin preparing the documentation for your applications. You will be in a position to complete and submit applications as soon as they become available in the fall.

Additionally, by taking the GMAT earlier rather than later, you build in a time cushion. If you plan to take the GMAT in the spring but circumstances prevent you from doing so, you can take the early-fall administration. Even though your score will not be available until six weeks later, your applications can still be submitted relatively early in the season. If you first schedule a GMAT administration in the early fall and are prevented from taking the test, the next opportunity won't be until the late fall. Your score won't be available until mid-January. As a consequence, your application will not be one of the first reviewed, and you may be ineligible for the early-decision programs offered by some schools.

You may take the GMAT more than once. In fact, you may take it several times. But our advice is: *Do it once, do it right, and don't do it again.* The basis for this advice is the reporting system. Your score report will show each time that you have taken the test and the result (a score or cancellation). Candidates routinely improve slightly on a second testing because of a "familiarity" factor, and admissions officers are aware of this. Furthermore, a single high score at the end of a string of otherwise disappointing performances would probably not be very impressive. Ideally, then, you want only your one, highest test score.

What if you have already taken the GMAT and received a disappointing score or perhaps scores? Would it then be advisable for you to take the test again? Unfortunately, there is no single, clear-cut answer to this question, because there is always the risk that another testing will result in the same or even a lower score. There are, however, circumstances that strongly suggest that another testing could be advantageous:

- External factors such as illness or emotional trauma interfered with your performance on the earlier test.

- A random event such as miscoding the answer sheet or drastic misallocation of time distorted your performance on the earlier test.

- Lack of adequate preparation prevented you from achieving your best performance on the earlier test.

Indeed, an admissions officer might be willing to discount an earlier, lower score if it can be explained in terms of external or random factors. (Don't try to explain a low score to an admissions officer by claiming "lack of adequate preparation"!)

Finally, if you simply must have a higher score to gain admission to a particular school that is your main target, then you obviously must take the test again. You should understand, however, that there is a point after which it just doesn't make sense to take the GMAT again. Even if you happen to have a particularly good day and improve dramatically, your chances for admission may not improve. If a business school admissions officer sees a string of low scores followed by a single good score, the single good score is likely to be regarded as an anomaly.

Note that ETS does not automatically inform business schools that a candidate is planning to take the GMAT another time. If you determine that it is necessary to retake the test, contact any schools at which you have applications pending. Explain that you are retaking the test, and ask them to delay any unfavorable action on your application until the results of the retesting are in.

Except for the issue of retesting, this advice would also apply to taking the TOEFL (if you will be required to submit a TOEFL score). Find out when the test is offered near you, and make sure that you schedule a session far enough in advance to ensure that your TOEFL score too will reach your target schools in plenty of time. Remember, also, that it may be necessary to retake the TOEFL if you fail to achieve a score that exceeds any minimum required by the various schools to which you are applying.

SPIN CONTROL

Although each business school develops its own application forms, the differences among them are not really very significant. All ask for essentially the same information.

The "Personal Data" form is designed to elicit the information that you would ordinarily include on your resume (though perhaps this particular form asks for greater detail) as well as some data that will be helpful to the staff of the admissions office. Forms such as this provide only limited space, so if your resume is fairly lengthy, you may want to attach additional sheets. Just make sure that you crossreference every additional page for the reader's easy access.

You may also find that you have to make some decisions about what to include as part of your responses and what to exclude. In terms of making a persuasive presentation, there is a danger in including too many items; it is not necessarily the case that more is better. This is particularly true if you have three or four major accomplishments or activities and several that are less significant. While a long list might at first seem to be impressive, it is not likely that you are going to be able to overwhelm an experienced admissions officer with sheer numbers. Rather, you should strive to *craft* an application that "hangs together." The information that you include on a Personal Data form (such as awards, accomplishments, activities, etc.) should support the conclusions that you reach in your personal statement and in your answers to any essay prompts. Ideally, your letters of recommendation should also support these aspects of your application.

Additionally, you should choose carefully the words that you use to describe what you have done; that is, you should make sure that you control the impression that you want the reader to come away with. Consider the following example from the Personal Data section for a business school applicant:

1990–93   Traffic Controller, Union Carbide

Without further explanation, the title "Traffic Controller" might suggest someone who directs vehicles into and out of the company parking lot. When questioned, the applicant explained that the traffic controller is responsible for making shipping arrangements for freight worth hundreds of millions of dollars each year and, further, that the position requires a thorough knowledge of complex government regulations regarding freight shipments and charges.

Most Personal Data forms will give you the opportunity to explain the significance of an achievement or accomplishment, so make sure that you utilize that opportunity. As you draft your explanations, keep in mind that you are more familiar with the events in question than the reader is. For example, the term "Traffic Controller" obviously had a very precise meaning for the applicant just mentioned, but its meaning was lost on us—and likely would have been lost on an admissions officer. Compare the following entries:

Bland: Traffic Controller
            Responsible for scheduling freight shipments.

Better: Traffic Controller
            Responsible for scheduling freight shipments worth $100 million each year to 100 plants and customers via truck, rail, and plane.

Bland: Personnel Coordinator
            Responsible for hiring researchers and lab assistants.

Better: Personnel Coordinator
            Responsible for interviewing and hiring scientific researchers (Ph.D. plus three years' lab experience required) and lab assistants for a division with 1,500 employees.

Bland: Regional Sales Manager
              Supervised thirty-five sales representatives.

Better: Regional Sales Manager
              *Created sales strategies for and supervised thirty-five
              sales representatives for a ten-state area producing a
              gross of $150 million annually.*

Both descriptive and quantitative details are very important to communicate this sort of information to a reader with some impact.

Another way of putting the right spin on your application is to make sure that you highlight any aspect of your achievements that might be of particular interest to an admissions officer (as opposed to a prospective employer or client). To do this, you should read the school's bulletin carefully to learn whether there is anything in your background that fits especially well with the school's description of its own objectives. For example, if a school boasts of its "international" dimension, then any aspect of your background that suggests that you might add to that dimension should be incorporated into the application.

Additionally, there are three general trends in the philosophy of graduate management study that you can try to align yourself with: globalization, teamwork, and public service. If you read the informational bulletins of several schools, you will likely find these concepts mentioned prominently. As for globalization, the theory is that political events (such as the dissolution of the Soviet Union and the creation of free markets in China) portend changes in the way that business is done: We are moving toward a global community in which the entire world (rather than this or that country) will be a business community. So, proficiency in a foreign language, significant travel experience, and knowledge of a different culture are now regarded as important positive factors in an application. The trend toward teamwork signals the end of the heyday of the individual and the dawn of an era of cooperative effort. Team players are in, and buckaroos are out, so adjust your descriptive remarks accordingly. Finally, in the wake of Watergate and other major scandals in government and business that followed it, business schools have become more concerned about the moral dimensions of graduate study in management. As a result, community service and volunteerism are now considered positive features of an application.

Of course, you have to be subtle in your attempt to align yourself with these trends. It would seem disingenuous, for example, to write, "I am a big believer in globalization, and as soon as I can find the time, I plan to study a foreign language and travel abroad." Obviously, this statement seems contrived and offered for the sole purpose of allowing the applicant to jump on the "globalization bandwagon." Your objective is to weave subtle mention of these factors into the fabric of the application so that they seem to be part of its warp and woof and not merely appliqués.

LETTERS OF RECOMMENDATION

As part of the application process, many business schools ask that applicants obtain two or three letters from outside parties in which these people comment on the applicant's background. Other schools don't require such letters but accept them if an applicant arranges for them. These letters are often referred to as letters of recommendation.

There are two widely held misconceptions about letters of recommendation. First, many people wrongly believe that the quality of a letter of recommendation is entirely a function of the title of the letter writer. Mention letters of recommendation to these people, and they immediately start reviewing a mental list of relatives, family friends, and long-forgotten casual acquaintances, searching for the names of prominent figures upon whom they might impose for a letter.

This "star-search" approach to choosing people to write letters of recommendation is misguided. Admissions officers are not particularly interested in learning that you are politically well connected. In fact, the star-search approach may backfire. One admissions officer tells of the letter that a school received from the vice-president of the United States. The applicant had evidently met the vice-president at some political rally and had enough clout within the party to get a letter of recommendation on the official letterhead of the vice-president of the United States. The gist of the letter follows:

> *To the Committee:*
>
> *I recommend this applicant for admission to your school. I met the applicant at an official function, and I was very impressed with his honest face and firm handshake.*
>
> *Sincerely,*
>
> *The Vice-President of the United States*

The letter had the unintended side effect of providing some amusement for the people in the admissions office, but it didn't advance the applicant's cause. In fact, the letter almost certainly hurt his chances. The applicant seemed to have been thinking, "The vice-president is so important, they'll have to accept me." But admissions officers don't have to take orders from a vice-president—not even the vice-president of the United States. The admissions officers at this school were understandably insulted that the applicant thought them so unsophisticated.

We do not mean to suggest that you should avoid obtaining letters of evaluation from prominent people. The fatal flaw in the letter above is not that it was written by the vice-president of the United States. Rather, the problem with the letter is that it says nothing relevant about the applicant. There is no basis for the conclusion that the school should accept the applicant. Later we will show you how to avoid this error.

The second common misconception about letters of recommendation is, in a way, the mirror image of the star-search fallacy. It finds voice in the common sentiment, "Don't bother with letters of recommendation. Business schools don't pay attention to them anyway." In fact, there may be a kernel of truth underlying this view. After all, what weight could be given to the kind of letter described above? Letters like that may explain why some business schools don't seem to be particularly enthusiastic about receiving letters of recommendation. The letters are so superficial and perfunctory that they are of no value whatsoever in evaluating an applicant.

Yet other schools do solicit and even insist upon letters of recommendation. Why? Because they know that a well-considered letter of recommendation from an appropriate source can refine their picture of an applicant. For those schools that solicit or require letters of recommendation, it is very important that you make every effort to secure effective letters and that you follow through to be certain that the letters are submitted before the deadline. Those schools that expect to see effective letters with each application may regard an application without a letter as "incomplete."

Even if a school doesn't require letters of recommendation, you should arrange to have yours sent there anyway. Paradoxically, an effective letter of recommendation may actually be very important at a school that seems less than enthusiastic about such letters. The fact that a school is not very interested in letters of recommendation may say something about the quality of letters that the school usually receives. If, by and large, the letters don't add anything to the admissions process, then you can understand why a school doesn't really want to be burdened with them. On the other hand, imagine that a school receives a very powerful letter. Since the other applicants have only perfunctory letters or none at all, the rare, very powerful letter of recommendation takes on even greater significance. In the same way that an application without effective letters looks defective to a school that requires such letters, at a school that does not require them the application with an effective letter really stands out.

What Makes an Effective Letter of Recommendation?

To start with, let's substitute the term "letter of evaluation" for "letter of recommendation." To be sure, you will want to make certain that your letter writers are favorable to your cause and "recommend" you for admission, but an effective letter must go beyond a simple recommendation. An effective letter contains an evaluation of the applicant's qualifications.

A good letter of evaluation has three important features:

1. It shows that the writer is someone who knows enough about intellectual ability and academic or professional effectiveness in general to make comparative judgments about the qualifications of the particular applicant.

2. It shows that the writer is someone who knows enough about the particular applicant to make an informed judgment about the applicant's qualifications.

3. It contains not only the writer's general conclusions about the applicant but enough supporting detail to make those conclusions believable.

Each of these features is essential. As for the first, for the letter to be effective, the writer must be able to provide some information about those qualities that bear on the applicant's ability to be a successful M.B.A. student and later an effective manager or entrepreneur. Obviously, a letter from someone in "business" is appropriate, and many business schools express a preference for this type of letter—particularly those schools that look for significant work experience. Also appropriate, however, would be a letter from a college professor, whose job it is to evaluate students. The key point to remember is simply that the person who writes the letter must have a perspective from which to make a meaningful evaluation.

The second requirement for an effective letter of evaluation is straightforward. Unless the letter writer has enough information about the applicant to form an opinion, then the letter simply won't be credible. And the forms supplied by many schools explicitly ask that the letter writer provide a context for the reader. Don't fall into the star-search trap. Your letters do not have to come from "captains of industry." You should prefer an immediate supervisor who knows the details of your work to a more remote superior who is not personally knowledgeable about your talents—even though the more remote superior may have an impressive title.

Sometimes an applicant may be reluctant to ask an employer for a letter of evaluation because the employer doesn't know that the employee is applying to business school, and the employee doesn't want the employer to know. Since this is a position of current employment, a business school will obviously be expecting a letter of evaluation covering this aspect of the applicant's professional life. The lack of such a letter may cause an admissions officer to draw a negative conclusion: The applicant couldn't find anyone to say something nice and so did not offer a letter.

If you find yourself in this position, then use a colleague or an outside business associate as the letter writer. The person you select for this purpose must satisfy the first requirement of a good letter writer—a basis for comparison. The technician who services your office's computer system may be an electronic wizard, but that alone doesn't qualify him to write a letter of evaluation to an admissions officer at a business school. But a professional colleague —someone who has professional responsibilities and might be expected to write the same sort of letter for a subordinate— easily fills the bill. You might even look outside of your firm. A client, for example, might be an appropriate choice.

As for the third requirement—sufficient detail—many business schools have created forms that force letter writers to offer very specific conclusions and to provide some sort of support for those conclusions.

In conclusion, then, there are no rigid rules about who should write letters of recommendation. Rather, your choice should be guided by your understanding of the function of these letters in the admissions process. Letters of recommendation—or, more precisely, letters of evaluation— should provide an independent assessment of your abilities. They should come from a writer who has a basis for making a comparison, who knows you as an individual well enough to make such a comparison, and who is willing to write a letter sufficiently detailed to be of value to an admissions committee.

INTERVIEWS

Many schools require a personal interview, either on or off campus. Schools that do not require an interview may nonetheless be willing to grant one. And even schools that discourage interviews might be willing to do one provided that an applicant can show good reason for a face-to-face meeting. What you can expect during an interview will depend on whether the interview is one requested or even required by the school or one that you have requested.

If you are requesting an interview from an admissions office that does not routinely use interviews as part of the decision-making process, then you had better have some good reason for requesting one. Unfortunately, some people have the mistaken impression that an interview is a sort of automatic pass to admission: "If they just sit down and talk to me, they will see that I am really a decent, caring, warmhearted human being, and they won't be able to turn me down." This reasoning is wrong. Unless you really have something to add to your written application, there is no reason to request an interview, and you run the risk that the interview will proceed along the following lines:

Applicant:	Hi, my name is I.M. Applicant.
Dean:	Pleased to meet you. I'm dean of admissions.
Applicant:	Yes, well?
Dean:	Yes?
Applicant:	Well?
Dean:	Yes?
Applicant:	Well, I'm here for my interview.
Dean:	Yes, you requested an interview. What would you like to tell me.
Applicant:	Uh, uh, uh . . .

If *you* request an interview, then it had better be because you have something to say in person that you could not make clear in the written application, and you had better have your presentation planned out.

When the interview is initiated by the admissions office, you know that you are going to be examined on the principal elements discussed in chapter 2: ability, motivation, and uniqueness. So the substantive agenda of the conversation is, in a sense, already established by the nature of the exercise. Additionally, your ability to think on your feet and to communicate effectively will be a background issue, and the interviewer will be taking mental notes on how you handle yourself. At issue also will be your credibility. Thus, the best advice is "Be prepared!"

"Be prepared" is at one and the same time both reassuringly simple advice and impossibly open-ended. On the one hand, you can anticipate that the interviewer will attempt to elicit from you information about ability and motivation. You can expect to hear specific questions about the information you have provided on the Personal Data forms. And you can expect to hear questions such as:

What are your reasons for applying to business school?

Why do you want to go to this business school?

What do you plan to do when you graduate?

What do you expect you will be doing ten years from now?

How do you think an M.B.A. is going to help you?

Since you presumably have given these issues a lot of thought while filling out the written portion of the application, these types of questions shouldn't pose much of a problem. It's a good idea, however, to organize your responses to these generic questions in advance. That way, you'll be able to answer coherently and confidently. Of course, this does not mean that you should script your answers and then memorize them, but it does mean that you should be prepared.

On the other hand, you may have an interviewer who delights in surprising applicants by asking off-the-wall questions such as:

Assume that you are stranded on a small tropical island. After a survey of the island you find that you have an ample supply of fresh water and plenty of fruits and plants for food. But there are no other humans on the island. What would you do in the first five days? In the first five months? In the first five years?

Obviously, the purpose of this question is not to elicit further information about the life events that you mention in your application, nor to stimulate a discussion about your reasons for applying to business school. Rather, this type of question (which unfortunately can degenerate into gamesmanship on the part of the interviewer) is designed to let the interviewer see how you think on your feet. And because of the nature of the inquiry, you cannot prepare for a specific question. If you get such a question, just make sure that your brain is in gear before you put your mouth into motion. You don't have to start talking immediately; in fact, taking a moment to reflect on the question will impress upon the interviewer that you are a person of judgment, someone who does not act precipitously. So take a deep breath and think for a few seconds before you respond.

In Conclusion

Chapter 2 analyzed the admissions process from the standpoint of the decision-maker. Now you should understand how to use that information in preparing your own application. Your ultimate goal is a well-crafted application—one that hangs together and addresses both explicitly and implicitly the issues of ability, motivation, and uniqueness. The next chapter presents what will be the keystone of your application: the personal statement.

THE PERSONAL STATEMENT: WHAT TO SAY

Many business schools invite you to submit, with your application, any additional information not already solicited by the application form that you think might be relevant. Others insist upon a written explanation of your reasons for applying to business school, and still others require essay responses to an elaborate system of prompts. The difference among these various requirements is not so much qualitative as quantitative. All are designed to elicit information about personal background (including family and education), special achievements or experiences, reasons for applying to business school, and professional goals and expectations.

A VARIETY OF PROMPTS

For ease of reference, an essay on any or all of the topics listed in the preceding paragraph, whether optional or required, will be referred to as a "personal statement." It must be acknowledged, however, that the use of the phrase "personal statement" tends to oversimplify matters some- what. Some applications do include general, open-ended invitations in words similar to the following examples:

> **If there is any other information that you feel is impor- tant to our assessment of your candidacy, feel free to add it to your application.**

> **Is there any additional information that you wish to provide the admissions committee?**
>
> **If there is further information that you believe would be helpful to the admissions committee, please feel free to provide it.**

This sort of invitation obviously contemplates submission of a written statement highlighting certain achievements or explaining unusual aspects of a candidate's background, and the phrase "personal statement" nicely captures the function of such statements. (These prompts also seem to leave the door open for submitting items other than a written essay, but the wisdom of submitting exhibits, artifacts, and other unusual objects will be discussed later in this chapter.)

While some applications include prompts that naturally lead to a general personal statement or essay about accomplishments and goals, others are designed to elicit more specific responses. Some prompts, for example, ask about significant accomplishments:

> **List your three most important achievements and explain why you consider them important.**
>
> **Describe any significant study, employment, or travel in the past five years.**
>
> **Tell us about one or two accomplishments in your life that are not mentioned elsewhere in this application. Why are you proud of them?**

Other application prompts ask for a discussion of career objectives:

> **Why are you seeking a degree from our business school?**
>
> **Elaborate on your future career plans and your motivation for pursuing a graduate degree at this business school.**
>
> **What are your tentative goals for the next five years of your life, and how do you see the M.B.A. helping you to reach them?**

Some applications include prompts that are designed to elicit personal information but that are cleverly crafted to stimulate applicant interest:

Tell us about a risk that you have taken in your life.

Imagine that, five years following graduation, your name appears in a "Who's Who" directory. What would you want the accompanying description to say?

The first of these prompts is designed to elicit information about past accomplishments, and the second aims at encouraging discussion of plans and goals. Thus, they are not different from the prompts above in what they hope to learn, but their format is designed to stimulate thoughtful responses.

All of the essay prompts presented above are concerned with personal information. A few business schools, however, either require or invite essays on substantive matters such as managerial strategies or business ethics:

Describe a significant problem faced by your company, your industry, or your community and outline the procedures you would follow to investigate and solve it.

You are the product manager for a line of pesticides that are used to protect stored grains. For the past several years, this line has accounted for a substantial portion of your company's income. Recently, however, an in-house study concluded that there is a possibility that these chemicals cause health problems in people who eat food products manufactured from grains treated with them, though such problems may not become apparent until someone has eaten a substantial quantity of such foods over a five- to ten-year period. You have complete authority in this situation. What are the issues that face your company, and what course of action do you recommend?

These last two prompts really do not ask for personal-statement responses. The first clearly asks for a substantive discussion of a real-world problem, and the second for an ethical analysis of a hypothetical problem. The answer to the first will depend on the candidate's previous managerial experience, and an answer to the second on the candidate's moral sensibilities. Because answers to such prompts are likely to be highly idiosyncratic, there is little concrete advice that can be offered on answering them. However, there is much to be gained from a discussion of personal-statement essays.

THE IMPORTANCE OF THE PERSONAL STATEMENT

When asked to name the most important part of the application, many admissions officers single out the personal statement. What they mean is this: "If a candidate is otherwise qualified in terms of GPA, GMAT, and work experience, then the personal statement becomes the most important factor in making a final decision on the application." In other words, an effective personal statement can provide an affirmative reason for accepting an application. A persuasive statement may even help a candidate overcome a relatively low GPA or GMAT score.

While the importance of the personal statement cannot be overstated, neither should this point be misconstrued. Admissions officers make it quite clear that even a powerfully written personal statement cannot save an application that is already doomed by a GPA or GMAT score that is significantly below the median numbers typically accepted. An effective personal statement may be the factor that most often distinguishes those applications with reasonably good quantitative factors that are accepted from similar applications that are rejected; however, the personal statement by itself—no matter how good—is not going to offset the negative effect of numbers that are simply too low.

If the personal statement is the most important part of the application from the standpoint of the admissions office, then it obviously should be treated as the most important part of the application from the applicant's perspective. It should be the centerpiece of the application—carefully crafted and dramatically exhibited, surrounded by the GMAT score, the GPA, letters of recommendation, employment history, and lists of achievements. In fact, admissions officers often describe the hallmark of a successful application in terms such as "It makes sense as a whole" or "It hangs together." The personal statement binds together all of the pieces of the application so that it makes a coherent whole.

There is another reason why you should regard the personal statement as the most important part of the application: It is the one part of the application over which you have any short-term control. By the time you begin submitting applications, virtually every aspect of the application other than the personal statement has already been determined. Your college marks (except perhaps for a single, final semester) have already been entered on your official transcript, your GMAT score has been calculated by ETS (subject, perhaps, to retaking the exam), and your work record and extracurricular and community activities are history. The personal statement, however, is yet to be written. You are still in control of its content, its organization, and its execution.

In spite of the critical importance of the personal statement—an importance attested to by admissions officers year in and year out—countless numbers of applicants apparently believe that the personal statement is just one more administrative burden that should be discharged as quickly as possible and with as little effort or inconvenience as possible. The statements written by these candidates reflect this attitude. They are usually ill-conceived and poorly executed, and they ultimately fail to advance the applicant's cause.

A weak personal statement is almost sure to compromise an applicant's chance for acceptance, as a moment's reflection will demonstrate. Imagine that you are an admissions officer and that you have before you two applications from individuals with comparable quantitative credentials and professional experience. One application includes a thoughtful, well-crafted personal statement, the other a personal statement that is superficial, poorly organized, and full of errors. As an admissions officer, you are relying on this additional information to make informed and intelligent admissions decisions. You would almost surely be disappointed in the effort of the second candidate and would be disinclined to act favorably on this application. You might even take umbrage at the fact that a person seeking admission to your institution didn't think it important to do a thorough job in completing your application form. You might understandably be disposed to reject the application whatever its other merits.

This tendency of applicants to slight the personal statement, however, is not confined to those candidates who might be ambivalent about the application process or just plain lazy. Even candidates who understand the importance of the personal statement often fail to derive maximum advantage from the opportunity it offers. Some fail to keep in mind the factors that admissions officers are looking for and so write statements that are inappropriate in various ways. Others are satisfied with a first or second draft and so stop too soon. Drafting and editing a compelling personal statement may take forty or fifty hours or even longer, depending on the extent of a candidate's professional experience and the complexity of the series of prompts in the application.

If you are really committed to two years of rigorous study (or the part-time equivalent) and truly want to get into the best business school you can, then you should be excited by the fact that you have the opportunity to write a personal statement that may make the difference between acceptance and rejection, and you should be willing to spend the long hours needed to bring it to its best form. On the other hand, if you really can't be bothered, then perhaps you really don't want to go to business school that badly.

WHAT TO SAY IN THE PERSONAL STATEMENT

What should you put in your personal statement? One way of answering that question is to say that you should tell admissions officers what they want to hear. And what do they want to hear? They want to hear about the qualities mentioned in chapter 2: ability, motivation, and uniqueness. Telling admissions officers what they want to hear doesn't mean filling your personal statement with flattering remarks about their institutions. Rather, it means creating a personal statement that demonstrates that your background and goals answer to the institutional needs that shape the admissions process. In other words, your personal statement should discuss your ability, your motivation, and your unique assets.

Of course, the content of a personal statement must respond to the specific demands of different prompts. Obviously, a discussion of your career objectives would not be an appropriate response to a prompt that asks about significant accomplishments, nor would a detailed personal history be a good answer to a question about career plans and goals. But a generic personal statement that discusses all three elements can be adapted to virtually any prompt. Consider this very general prompt used on many application forms: "Tell us anything about yourself that might be relevant." This prompt invites you to discuss anything that bears on the issues of ability, motivation, and uniqueness. A generic personal statement that effectively responds to this general prompt can be adapted for virtually all other prompts.

Crafting a generic personal statement is a valuable prelude to preparing any business-school application. It will include language, facts, and arguments that will respond to open-ended prompts in actual applications. The content of a generic personal statement can also be adapted to meet the demands of prompts that require more limited responses, such as a discussion of past achievements or an outline of career plans. The generic personal statement outlined below is an argument for your admission to business school. It has the following structure:

I. I have the ability to succeed in business school and later as a manager.

    A. My previous academic success proves this point.

    B. My employment history proves this point.

    C. My extra achievements prove this point.

II. I am committed to succeeding in business school and later as a manager.

    A. This is a well-considered decision.

    B. My career plans are formed.

III. I have something unique to contribute to my business-school class.

You will observe that this format flows naturally from the admissions factors discussed in chapter 2. Admissions officers want to hear about ability, motivation, and uniqueness—so you should tell them just that.

One significant advantage of this format is that it almost guarantees that your personal statement will be organized and easy to follow. It is important to keep in mind, however, that the personal statement should not simply repeat information that is available elsewhere in the standard application form. Imagine that you are an admissions officer and that you receive the following personal statement:

Tell us anything about yourself that you think might be relevant to our consideration of your application.

I want to use this additional space to demonstrate to the admissions committee that I have the ability to complete the school's curriculum, that I am highly motivated, and that I have something special to contribute to the learning atmosphere at the school.

First, I believe that my background shows that I have the ability to handle a challenging business school curriculum. Two years ago, I graduated from State University with a 3.36 grade point average with a major in psychology. Since then, I have been employed by Management Resources, Inc. While I was in college, I was vice-president of the Accounting Club, and for the past six months I have been treasurer of our town's Community Services Organization.

Second, I see the M.B.A. as the next logical step in my career. At Management Resources, I have been given greater and greater managerial responsibility, and I now realize that if I hope to go higher, I must have more formal training in management. After graduating from business school, I would expect to return to Management Resources for two or three years to gain further experience in consulting, but ultimately I plan to open my own consulting firm that would specialize in psychological profiling of workers.

Third, and finally, I believe that I have something unusual to contribute to a business school class. While in college, I worked summers at the Pleasant Valley Mental Hospital.

This personal statement does have the advantage of being well organized, but it is really not very interesting. In fact, it suffers from three major weaknesses. First, it simply repeats information that is already available in other parts of the application. Take, for example, the discussion of ability. The personal statement contains nothing more than what must already be available to the reader on the standardized application form:

I graduated two years ago. I have a 3.36 GPA. I majored in psychology. I work for Management Resources, etc.

Would an admissions officer really be impressed by a restatement of information already available in other parts of the application? Hardly! From the point of view of an admissions officer, the reason for a personal statement is to get information that is not otherwise available.

A second weakness of the essay is that it fails to explain the significance of the particular facts that it discusses. A personal statement should help an admissions officer interpret the data that complete the standardized application form. Missing from the sample personal statement above is any discussion of the *significance* of the various facts mentioned. Again, put yourself in the position of an admissions officer. The candidate writes:

I have a 3.36 GPA.

What does that mean? Is that good or is that bad? To be sure, as an admissions officer, you would know whether a 3.36 GPA is above or below the median GPA of this year's applicant pool; but what does that tell you? Is a 3.36 GPA the best work the candidate could hope to do, so that the candidate may not really be a very promising prospect? Is the candidate a chronic underachiever, so that you should worry whether the candidate will take business school seriously? Is the 3.36 an outstanding performance when viewed in light of the candidate's background? What these and other questions that we might ask tell us is that the naked fact that the candidate earned a certain GPA in college is the beginning rather than the end of the story.

Finally, a third weakness of the personal statement above is that it fails to take advantage of the one opportunity that the applicant has to influence the admissions officer and the admissions committee. In the mind of an admissions officer, this sample essay will be regarded as a liability when it is compared with better statements submitted by other applicants with similar backgrounds.

Contrast the treatment of the GPA in the sample personal statement above with the following:

> The committee will see from my transcript that I graduated from college with a 3.36 GPA, but that number understates my true academic ability for several reasons. First, I started out as a pre-med student but later discovered that I simply did not have the science background needed for the program. As a result, my GPA for my freshman year was only 2.88, but after I changed to psychology, my GPA was 3.66. Second, most semesters I held down part-time jobs, working anywhere from fifteen to twenty hours a week, and the need to support myself obviously took time away from my studies. Finally, although there is no official endorsement on the transcript, I nearly qualified for a double major. I was just one course short of a second major in French when I graduated.

From the perspective of an admissions officer, this second piece is much more interesting. First, it introduces information that is not available elsewhere in the application. Second, it explains the significance of the data for the reader. Finally, it makes a case for the applicant's acceptance.

The whole point of the personal statement is to introduce new information and explain its significance in such a way that it moves an admissions officer to act favorably on the application. There are several techniques to accomplish this goal that are available to almost every applicant.

One way to explain the significance of your GPA is to "recalculate" it in any of several ways. Consider the following examples:

> My final GPA for all four years of college is lower than it might otherwise have been because of my disappointing freshman year. My GPA for my last three years is 3.65, and for my senior year it is 3.8.

Or:

> I believe that I am a better student than my 3.4 GPA indicates. My GPA for my major area, which included several demanding courses, is 3.7.

Or:

> Although my undergraduate GPA is a bit low, I earned a 3.85 in graduate school and passed all three qualifying exams for my masters degree in psychology with highest honors.

Or:

> My final GPA was 3.5, but it would have been higher had I not had a very bad semester in my sophomore year because of the death of my mother.

A similar technique can be applied to your curriculum:

> Although my major was psychology, a quick look at my transcript will show that I took seven courses in philosophy. Had I not wanted to graduate on time, I could have taken another course in philosophy to complete a double major.

Or:

> I earned my degree in English literature in my college's Honors Program. All Honors Program courses require a term paper at least fifteen pages long.

Or:

> Psychology 402 was taught in the graduate school, and un-
> dergraduates were admitted to the course only with the
> professor's permission. I was one of only five undergradu-
> ates accepted for the seminar and the only one to get an A for
> the course.

The second element of the "ability" contention focuses on professional achievements. Here you need to describe the responsibilities you have been given, because an admissions officer will not necessarily understand the significance of your position just from the title. (Recall the discussion of the "traffic controller" in chapter 4.) A similar approach should be taken to any description of extracurricular or community activities. It is not enough to write, "In 1993, I was the chair of the Committee to Save Crandall Park." A fuller explanation is needed:

> In 1993, the city announced that due to fiscal pressures it
> would close Crandall Park, a fifty-acre facility with a swim-
> ming pool, a pond, and other recreational facilities situated in
> a lower-income neighborhood. I organized and was elected
> chair of the Committee to Save Crandall Park. The committee
> got nearly two dozen local merchants to donate over $125,000
> in cash and equipment for the preservation of the park. The
> committee then persuaded various civic organizations to take
> on maintenance tasks such as sweeping and trash collection
> on a rotating basis. These commitments have been renewed
> for each subsequent year, and the park remains open.

This is also a good example of how a generic personal statement can be adapted for other prompts. The description of the Committee to Save Crandall Park would fit very nicely into a response to a prompt such as "What are your three most significant accomplishments?"

The second major contention of the argument for admission deals with motivation, and for this part to be credible you will have to be specific. You should observe that the second contention has two parts. In the first part, you should explain how you came to the decision to pursue an M.B.A., and in the second you should sketch your plans for the first few years after you get the M.B.A. You may derive some guidance on this part from one of the prompts given at the beginning of this chapter:

What are your tentative goals for the next five years of your life, and how do you see the M.B.A. degree helping you to reach them?

A thoughtful answer to this prompt would provide good development for the second contention of your argument for admission, because it will both explain why you want an M.B.A. and what it will do for you.

Finally, since admissions officers are trying to create classes that include students with diverse backgrounds and different perspectives, you should comment on any unusual aspect of your background, including any outside interests that you may have.

How to Say It

As noted above, writing the personal statement is neither an easy task nor one that can be executed overnight. You should begin by considering carefully what you want to say. For inspiration, you may want to review the variety of prompts given at the beginning of this chapter. They will remind you of what admissions officers want to know about an applicant—for example, important accomplishments, short-term and long-term goals, and outside interests. Next, organize your thoughts into a coherent whole using the outline for a generic personal statement. Then, you should write your generic personal statement without regard to length. In your first draft, include everything that you would like an admissions committee to know.

Be aware, however, that if you follow this plan, your personal statement will almost surely be too long. It will contain ideas that are relatively unimportant when compared with other ideas. The mention of a minor award received during your freshman year in college will look out of place next to an award for academic achievement received as a senior, and a description of a summer job from years ago will probably pale in comparison to the full-time position you held after college graduation. So you should edit the statement for balance. Make sure that you don't have too many minor points that take away from the impact of the truly significant accomplishments and events. Then edit the statement carefully with regard to style, length, and grammar.

Your writing style is, of course, your own and is already well established, but there are a couple of general points you should keep in mind as you write your personal statement. First, you should avoid the temptation to dress up the statement with big words in an attempt to sound erudite. Consider some sentences from a personal statement that makes this error:

> I have always maintained a great interest in our commercial system and have always had the propensity to obtain a master's degree in business administration. However, due to several personal misfortunes in my household, I have not had the opportunity to apply to and attend business school until the present time.
>
> I am convinced that my personal and professional background would add immeasurably to your school's diversity, and I firmly believe that my demonstrated graduate academic successes are much more indicative of my scholastic capabilities than the undergraduate work I completed three years ago. Those successes, in conjunction with my GMAT score and my pertinent work experience, should make me an ideal candidate.

Commercial system? Propensity? Personal misfortunes? Household? Scholastic capabilities? Pertinent? The language is strained and makes the writer sound pompous and insincere. You'll fare better if you just express your thoughts directly and in your own words.

Second, avoid the temptation to overstate your case. The statement above asserts that the candidate has *always* been interested in pursuing an M.B.A. Always? Even before high school? And the statement claims that the applicant is an *ideal* candidate who would contribute immeasurably to the school. Ideal, as in perfect? And a contribution that cannot even be measured?

Obviously, the writer meant "for a long time" rather than "always" and a "strong candidate with an interesting background" rather than "ideal candidate who would contribute immeasurably." But then why not simply use the appropriate words? As written, those sentences are likely to alienate an admissions officer.

Third, many applicants worry that their personal statements sound a little too self-congratulatory. Everyone faces the same dilemma. On the one hand, you have to blow your own horn, and the personal statement is the appropriate forum for saying good things about yourself. On the other hand, there is real danger that an essay that contains too many "I" sentences will strike a discordant note in the reader. One way of escaping from this dilemma is to find ways of rewriting "I" sentences. This is not easy but it can be done. Compare the following excerpts from a personal statement by an applicant who, while a senior in college, had been chosen to play one of a series of student concerts with a major orchestra. First, the "I" version:

> One of my most significant accomplishments was being the guest soloist with the City Philharmonic. I had studied the piano since I was a child, and I was chosen by judges who were professional musicians from 100 pianists after three rounds of competition. During the concert, I played the Rachmaninov Piano Concerto in E Minor. This concerto is very difficult, and I practiced it for days and days. As I walked out on the stage the night of the concert, I was applauded by more than 500 people, and that is very exciting. After my performance, I received a standing ovation.

Now let's look at the same essay as rewritten to eliminate most of those "I" sentences:

> One of my most significant accomplishments was performing as guest soloist with the City Philharmonic. That performance represented the climax of many years of diligent study and practice, effort that was recognized by the professional musicians who acted as judges, choosing just one pianist from among 100 contestants after three rounds of competition. Imagine the thrill of walking onto a stage to the applause of 500 people. There are no words to describe the satisfaction that came from playing Rachmaninov's Piano Concerto in E Minor, one of the most difficult in the repertoire, with 75 professional musicians and having this accomplishment recognized by a standing ovation.

After careful editing only a single "my" remains. How was this transformation accomplished? By hard work. Unfortunately, there is no set formula that would allow you to purge your personal statement of all "I" sentences, but, as the example proves, if you are willing to spend some time editing your work you should be able to arrive at a statement that strikes an appropriate balance.

The second version is also likely to be more attractive to admissions officers, because it implicitly acknowledges that the performance of a piano concerto cannot be accomplished by a single person, even though the pianist is a soloist. As the revised version makes clear, the concert was a team effort; and business schools are looking for "soloists" who are able to play with a "team." Again, there is no way of prescribing how to implant this subliminal message in your essay. The best suggestion is that even as you work to identify and describe your important accomplishments, you should also recognize the extent to which they depended on the efforts of others.

Finally, careful editing can help contain the overall length of the personal statement. As you edit for length, you must consciously ask yourself, "Do I really need this word or phrase?" If the answer is no, then delete it. Editing for length is exacting detail work. Consider an example:

> My spouse and I have decided to move from New York and relocate to the Los Angeles area. We hold the opinion that California is the region of the country where we want to raise our family and where we both will be able to realize our professional goals and aspirations.

Does this statement really need the following:

> move from New York and
>
> We hold the opinion that
>
> the region of the country
>
> and aspirations

Those words can be deleted without sacrificing any of the content of the paragraph:

> My spouse and I have decided to relocate to the Los Angeles area. California is where we want to raise our family and where we will both be able to realize our professional goals.

SAYING IT CORRECTLY

You will obviously want to make sure that your personal statement is free of grammatical mistakes and other errors of expression. Here is a checklist that will help you to avoid errors that all too often remain in personal statements even after editing.

Check for Agreement between Subjects and Verbs

For every clause, identify the subject and the verb and make sure that they agree. Modifiers that separate the verb from the subject can obscure a problem of agreement.

> The highest officers of a large, multinational corporation has the power to bring about positive social change.

> A business school that offers a wide range of internship programs are particularly attractive since I plan to start my own business after I graduate.

In both sentences, there is a lack of agreement between subject and verb:

> officers . . . has

> business school . . . are

The plausibility of the incorrect verb choice, and therefore the chance that the error will go unnoticed because it "sounds right," is strengthened by a word or phrase near the verb that can be mistaken for the subject:

> corporation has

> programs are

You can avoid this type of oversight by isolating each and every subject and verb and checking for agreement.

Make Sure Each Pronoun Refers to a Particular Noun—and That the Two Agree in Number

A pronoun is used as a substitute for a noun. The noun it replaces is called its antecedent or referent. With the exception of certain idioms such as "It is raining," a pronoun that does not have a referent is used incorrectly.

> In my first year in college, I was not a very serious student, and because of it my overall average is not as high as it might otherwise have been.

> Many segments of our society do not have access to adequate medical care, which is what I plan to help remedy.

In the first sentence, the pronoun "it" lacks a referent. "It" needs to refer to something like "poor performance," but there is no such noun phrase in the sentence. The sentence needs to be rewritten:

> In my first year in college, I was not a very serious student; because of my poor first-year grades, my overall average is lower than it might otherwise have been.

In the second sentence, the relative pronoun "which" lacks a referent. "Which" seems to refer to something like "problem" or "situation," but no such word appears in the sentence. Use a noun:

> Many segments of our society do not have access to adequate medical care, and this lack of care is a problem that I plan to help remedy.

Additionally, a pronoun must agree with its referent in number:

> Today, a corporate president is likely to be a white, Anglo-Saxon, Protestant male, but in the future they will come from all types of backgrounds.

The pronoun "they" refers to "president," and the pronoun is plural while the noun is singular. The sentence can be corrected by making the noun plural:

> Today, corporate presidents are likely to be white, Anglo-Saxon, Protestant males, but in the future they will come from all types of backgrounds.

Make Similar Sentence Elements Parallel

Make sure that the elements of a sentence that perform similar or equal functions are presented in parallel form.

> At most colleges, the dominant attitude among students is that gaining admission to a professional graduate school is more important than to obtain a well-rounded education.

> The professor's review of our project was very favorable, citing the unusual photography, the complex plot, and the dialogue was very interesting.

In the first sentence, "gaining admission" and "to obtain" must both have the same form: "gaining admission is more important than obtaining." In the second sentence, each element in the series of features should have the same form: "citing the unusual photography, the complex plot, and the interesting dialogue."

Be Sure All Split Constructions Are Complete

Another error to avoid is incomplete constructions such as these:

> The committee's investigation revealed that the Department Head not only knew but encouraged the policy of using graduate assistants to grade final exams.

> I have in the past and will in the future work to ensure that corporations act in an environmentally responsible manner.

> For some people, earning a top salary is as important, if not more important than, making a meaningful contribution to society.

In each of these sentences, there is an error involving a split construction. In the first sentence, there is a missing preposition. The Department Head did not know the policy itself; rather the Department Head knew of the policy: "not only knew of but encouraged." In the second sentence, the error is in the verb. The auxiliary verb "have" needs the verb "worked," but "worked" does not appear in the sentence. The sentence can be corrected by completing the construction: "have in the past worked and in the future will work." In the third sentence, the error is an incomplete comparison. The sentence should read: "as important *as*, if not more important than."

Make Sure That Your Sentences Say What You Mean

Consider the following examples:

> The average salary of a top government official is much lower than the top-level management of most private corporations.

This sentence makes an illogical comparison because, as written, it attempts to compare money and people: "salary is lower than management."

The sentence actually means to compare one salary with another: "is lower than that of the top-level management."

Another common error is the infamous dangling modifier:

> Having just completed a graduate degree in biology, a career in the area of environmental protection offers me the best opportunity for professional advancement.

The sentence as written implies that the "career" has just completed a graduate degree in biology. The sentence must be rewritten:

> Because I have just completed a graduate degree in biology, a career in the area of environmental protection offers me the best opportunity for professional advancement.

Here is one final example of illogical expression:

> I received the Fuller Scholarship because my score on the qualifying exam was higher than that of any applicant.

This sentence makes the illogical assertion that the writer's score was higher than every score—including itself. The proper comparison would be:

> I received the Fuller Scholarship because my score on the qualifying exam was higher than that of any other applicant.

Eliminate All Split Infinitives

Check for split infinitives and rewrite sentences to avoid awkward construction:

> Because I know how to efficiently and effectively use time, I will be able to successfully complete business school.

The sentence should be rewritten:

> Because I know how to use time efficiently and effectively, I will be able to complete business school successfully.

BELLS AND WHISTLES

Since a business school may receive many more applications than it can possibly accept, you obviously need to make sure that yours stands out from the crowd. A question quite naturally arises about the wisdom of including exhibits or of doing something bizarre to catch the eye of the admissions committee. There is no single, uniquely correct answer to this question, and whether it would be a good idea to include additional "bells and whistles" with your application depends on what you have in mind.

Admissions officers tell of a variety of strategies applicants have used to gain attention. Some worked; others didn't.

One applicant placed the completed application, including the personal statement, into the arms of a life-sized cardboard figure of a person with a cutout photograph of the applicant's face on the head of the figure and sent the whole thing to the admissions office. That worked. Another applicant prepared a collage of magazine photos depicting various newsworthy events about business and commerce and sent the collage to the admissions office. That didn't work.

Another applicant, an architect, included a set of plans for a building. That worked. Another composed a song entitled "The Ballad of My Life" and submitted a recording of the song in lieu of a written personal statement. That didn't work.

Yet another applicant, who had received an acceptance from Harvard and a rejection from Stanford and who really wanted to study at Stanford, called the Stanford admissions office:

Applicant: This is Ima Applicant. A terrible mistake has been made. I just got a letter of rejection.

Clerk: Let me check the files. No, Ms. Applicant, no mistake was made. The dean rejected your application.

Applicant: I know. That's the mistake I'm talking about. I'll be on the next plane out there to help you sort this out.

Clerk: That won't be necessary. The dean has already made a final decision.

Applicant: See you in a couple of hours. Bye.

This story had a happy ending. The applicant managed to persuade the dean that Stanford had indeed made a mistake. Once admitted, the applicant subsequently graduated from Stanford at the top of the class, and went on to a successful career in real estate. Another applicant telephoned an admissions office and asked the dean to look out of the window at a nearby street corner. The dean did and saw a tent pitched on the corner of a busy intersection. The applicant explained over the phone that the camp would remain there—occupied around the clock by the applicant—until an acceptance was forthcoming. This stunt did not work.

What these anecdotes suggest is that at least some admissions officers look favorably on unusual applications. (Which is not to say that the applicants who were accepted would not have been accepted in any event.) But for bells and whistles to be effective, your application has to be competitive. A top business school is not going to accept an application with a rock-bottom GMAT score and GPA simply because the candidate makes them laugh. Still, an additional submission can help your application to stand out.

Certainly, you might want to include a representative sample of your work—for example, an article that you published, a part of an honors thesis or other paper that you wrote in school, or a successful grant proposal that you prepared. One factor an admissions officer will be looking for in applicants is the ability to communicate effectively, so a sample of your writing would be appropriate. Just make sure that the additional submission does not confuse or burden the reader. Make it clear that the additional exhibit is in addition to everything that is required by the admissions committee, that it doesn't require special care or treatment, and that you don't want it back. Given those safeguards, the worst that an admissions officer would likely do is simply throw out the additional material and read the required submissions.

It is also possible to submit exhibits other than writing samples, such as a photograph of a construction project that you managed, an audiotape of a musical performance (for an opera singer who wanted to go into arts management), or even a videotape of a presentation that you made at a recent sales conference. Just make sure that the additional submission bears on the issues discussed in chapter 2, and make it clear to the admissions officers that they have no obligation to preserve it.

Beyond these suggestions, an imaginative applicant might think of even more unusual exhibits. Keep in mind, though, that outlandish schemes can backfire. Before you try anything really crazy, you should probably run the idea by two or three friends—just to make sure that you are not about to commit application suicide.

IN CONCLUSION

The personal statement (or statements) should be the keystone of your application. Its importance cannot be overemphasized. It is your opportunity to argue your case to the admissions committee, so make sure that you use it to advance your cause. Finally, make the commitment to spending the time necessary to edit your personal statement carefully so that the result is a well-crafted centerpiece. The next chapter provides "before" and "after" looks at some sample personal statements.

FIVE PERSONAL STATEMENTS THAT WORKED

This chapter provides an inside look at the metamorphosis that a personal statement must undergo before it is finally submitted to a business school. For each of the examples in this chapter, you'll see a draft version—not a first draft, but rather one on which the writer has already done considerable rewriting and editing. Following the draft version, you will see critical comments. And after the critical comments, you will find a final version.

As you study these examples, keep three points in mind. First, the final versions may not be perfect, but they are considerable improvements over the drafts. Second, although only two versions are shown, these personal statements actually underwent several revisions. Third, try to notice the subtle changes in style and grammar that were made between the draft and final versions.

Personal Statement 1—Draft Version

Is there any additional information that you would like to provide to the Committee?

The study of business is challenging, exciting, and directly relevant to my future ambitions. In the next few paragraphs, I intend to explain and justify my belief that I would contribute to the learning environment and diversity of the business school's student body.

I grew up as one of nine children on a dairy farm in a very rural area. My parents taught their children the value of self-discipline, hard work, and personal initiative. I excelled academically in high school, ranking 8/57, and qualified as Governor's Scholar, Who's Who, and other academic awards.

I attended a nationally acclaimed engineering school at Georgia Tech. While attending this university, I worked between twenty and twenty-five hours each week to support myself. I graduated with an electrical engineering degree while paying for 100 percent of my education and living expenses. Though my undergraduate record is not outstanding, my grades do show a rising trend during my last two years. I was also able to make the dean's list one semester during which I decreased hours of employment.

Since I graduated from college, I have been employed in the Nuclear Power Division of the Union Power Company. In my position of employment, I have gained broad experience in the areas of engineering, personnel, and finance and have been promoted to positions of increasingly higher levels of responsibility. I have had experience in managing large projects from design to implementation. I have moved out of the strictly technical career path followed by many engineers to take promotions in the areas of personnel and management.

I currently represent Union Power Company in a joint venture undertaken by fifteen utilities with nuclear power plants to create a national employee database for the nuclear industry to draw upon. As committee chairman, I am responsible for the implementation of a significant portion of the system.

I also use my employment to enhance my public-speaking and writing abilities. Recently, I was chosen to participate in a company video training program, and I have also made presentations at many management training seminars and have published articles in company newsletters. As head of the interdepartmental Quality and Productivity team, I have found ways to improve the efficiency and effectiveness of many company programs. As one of the more respected and successful teams within the company, we have several times been recognized by the company with achievement awards.

Developing new programs that require the coordination of personnel from diverse fields is exhilarating and has required persistence, organization, and motivation.

Another indication of my motivation and persistence is my graduate degree. Five years ago, I completed an M.A. in nuclear engineering by attending school part-time. My performance in this program portends future academic success in business school. I graduated from this quality M.A. program with a GPA of 3.84. While in the M.A. program, I sharpened my analytical and research skills. One of the research projects I worked on was potentially going to be published in an academic journal.

To be well rounded, it is not only important to consider yourself and your career but also the needs of the community. I am involved with a number of civic organizations that have promoted social good. These include the Citizens Committee on Poverty in Washburn County, in which I hold the position of treasurer of the board of directors.

During my employment at Union Power, I have developed admiration for the utility industry and an awareness of its needs. There are many societal dilemmas that impact the utility and especially the nuclear industry. These dilemmas include: (1) the question of nuclear safety and the growing need for power, (2) the question of the need for a highly trained work force, and (3) the international versus parochial concerns of the industry. Having an M.B.A. would help me contribute to solving these problems.

CRITIQUE

This personal statement needs considerable editing. The primary weakness of the statement is its lack of any overall organizing theme. The first half of the statement follows a chronological order, but then the chronology breaks down, and points seem to be strung together in no particular order. Because the points are not arranged around a theme such as ability or motivation, the potential persuasive effect of the statement is never realized.

Additionally, the statement is at least twice as long as it needs to be. Even when the statement makes points that are important, the language is needlessly wordy and awkward. And the statement includes irrelevant information and information that, while relevant, is already included in the application form. The problem of length is at least partially a result of the lack of organization. If a statement lacks a guiding theme, there is a strong temptation to toss in any point that seems to be interesting.

This statement should be reorganized around the three factors that the reader will be looking for. This candidate's professional accomplishments and recent academic work demonstrate ability. The drift in professional development away from the technical side of the industry to the managerial side shows the motivation for applying to business school. And the volunteer work provides the uniqueness factor.

Most of the first three paragraphs should be eliminated. The praise of graduate management education as an institution is gratuitous, and the candidate's high-school achievements are no longer relevant. From the third paragraph, the point about working part-time as an undergraduate should be salvaged, and the rest of the essay should be organized around the following four points:

- description of writer's career path

- description of responsibilities assumed

- importance of graduate study

- significance of volunteer work

Let's try to weave these strands together into a whole statement that shows that the candidate has the qualifications that an admissions officer is looking for.

Personal Statement 1—Final Version

Is there any additional information that you would like to provide to the committee?

Since graduating from college, I have worked for the Nuclear Power Division of Union Power Company. Because my undergraduate degree was in electrical engineering, I initially entered upon a technical career path with Union Power. Over the past few years, however, I have moved steadily away from the technical side of the industry toward the personnel and management side. An M.B.A. seems to be the logical extension of this career path. Formal training in management practices coupled with my technical background would better enable me to handle the management issues that are unique to the nuclear power industry.

As my resumé shows, I have already been given increasingly important responsibilities in these areas. My present assignment is to represent Union Power in a joint venture that includes fifteen nuclear utilities. The objective of the venture is to develop a national employee database for the nuclear industry to draw upon. The committee, of which I am the chair, is designing a certification process to ensure that key positions in the industry are filled by properly trained, competent, and reliable workers.

I understand that my college GPA is somewhat low. I would point out, however, that I worked twenty to twenty-five hours each week during the academic year and that I graduated with absolutely no indebtedness. A better indicator of my academic ability is the GPA that I earned while getting an M.A. in nuclear engineering. Also, I was recently chosen to participate in a company video training program, and I have enclosed a brief excerpt of my participation in the program so that the committee might assess my ability as a speaker.

Finally, the committee should know that I was one of nine children raised on a dairy farm in a very rural area. The daily hardships faced by my parents made a lasting impression. The Citizens Committee on Poverty in Washburn County, of which I am the treasurer, designs and funds programs to reduce the incidence of poverty in Washburn County. One of the Committee's programs, which was my idea, is the College Funding Program. The CFP searches college catalogues nationwide for unusual scholarships. Last year, because of CFP's efforts, six Washburn High School seniors, who otherwise probably could not have afforded to go to college, were able to continue their education.

Personal Statement 2—Draft Version

Please submit a double-spaced, typewritten statement of no more than two pages explaining why the committee should accept your application.

I have chosen your business school because of the noted specialty it offers in international business as the place where I would most like to receive my business school education. My ability to succeed is illustrated by my academic record and challenging curriculum as an undergraduate at the university's School of International Studies, my strong research and communications skills at various selected internships and employment, as well as by my dedication to the university's community.

This May, I will graduate with a 3.7 grade point average in my major, International Politics, from the David Thorpe School of International Studies. I received dean's list honors my last two years as I chose courses that interested me in the field of International Politics such as International Law, Crises in South American Relations, and Political Geography. I also passed the required Spanish Proficiency examination which tested not only my fluency and command of the Spanish language but also my knowledge of Spain and Latin America in the areas of politics, economics, and history. Despite my average GMAT score, I believe that my academic honors and my challenging curriculum show that I have the ability to face the rigorous case loads and demands expected at the business school.

My courses in my major required extensive research, and I became confident in writing large term papers each semester. Being on the East Coast, it was possible to travel to Washington, D.C., to do firsthand research by personally communicating with foreign embassies, American and foreign business, and international organizations. I learned to find and cultivate primary sources in addition to secondary sources. These research skills are necessary for business school. For example, I wrote a paper entitled "The Effect of Hierarchical Organization on Intelligence Agencies: The Decision to Support the Invasion of Cuba."

My various internships demanded research also. I spent one summer interning for the National Journalism Center in an academically accredited program. I gathered materials on airline deregulation at the Library of Congress and various Senate committee offices. My research culminated in my drafting a paper on airline deregulation and contributing to a series of articles appearing in *The Tribune.* This research experience should be a significant help to me for the preparation of papers and case studies required in business school.

Interning for Martin, Collier and Taft (a consulting firm) my senior year of college, I worked exclusively for a partner who was one of my professors at the university. I prepared reports for the firm's clients. In these reports I analyzed the issues, developments, and implications for United States businesses on what to expect from the emergence of the European Economic Community. I also drafted and edited articles for the firm's client newsletter on the new federal government legislation dealing with international cases of commerce and trade. Interpreting and explaining these complex issues has helped me to familiarize myself with the important concepts that business schools teach.

Wanting to give something back to the student community, I joined the Women's Caucus. During my senior year, as vice-president of the organization, I organized and led a campaign to secure university financing for on-campus child care for the families of university employees. The facility now provides full-time child care for twenty children. I believe that this experience strengthened my commitment to family values.

Continuing my desire to hold a leadership position, I became active in the student body at the university. I was chosen as a class representative my junior and senior years and planned special events and organized various class committees. I had to allocate my time carefully to handle my challenging schedule, and I believe that this self-discipline is the key to success in business school.

Business has always been a part of my life, and my familiarity with international business began when my father would return home from his travels abroad on behalf of the company he worked for. My interest in international business led me to take courses in my major field. My internship with the consulting firm and my friendship with one of the partners furthered my desire to learn more.

CRITIQUE

Let's begin this critique with a question: Were you able to read the entire statement? This is the classic "overachiever" personal statement. (Being an overachiever is not necessarily bad, but writing a statement about yourself that is too long is not good.) It is to guard against statements like this that the prompt places a two-page limit on the submission.

This statement also deserves more particular criticisms. First, it is too "busy." Some events in your life are more important than others, and you will have to choose to highlight some and ignore others. For example, the mention of the father in the final paragraph seems unwarranted.

Second, the statement is not organized around a central theme. It is simply a series of anecdotes strung together, punctuated by conclusions about what might be important in business school.

Third, the statement is "preachy." The writer keeps telling the business-school admissions officer what skills are needed for graduate study in management. But business school admissions officers already know what skills they are looking for. The personal statement should exhibit the skills and leave it to the admissions officers to draw the appropriate conclusions. In fact, simply deleting every sentence that explains what the admissions officer should be looking for will shorten the statement considerably.

Finally, the statement repeats a lot of information already included in the application form. For example, the writer doesn't need to repeat the name "David Thorpe School of International Studies." That information is presumably included in the Personal Data portion of the application.

Personal Statement 2—Final Version

Please submit a double-spaced, typewritten statement of no more than two pages explaining why the committee should accept your application.

I am applying to your business school because I want to pursue a career in international business. Next semester, I will graduate with at least a 3.7 grade point average in my major, International Politics, and I have already passed the department's Oral Proficiency Exam in Spanish. The exam tests not only fluency in Spanish but also knowledge of the politics, economics, and history of Spain and Latin America.

Most of the courses in the Department of International Politics require a least one major paper on a topic approved in advance by the professor, and the department's professors encourage students to research a narrow question in depth rather than to write generally and superficially about some large event. Thus, I learned to burrow deeply into the library to find the transcript of a hearing held by an obscure Congressional subcommittee or an editorial in a Spanish-language newspaper. To give the committee a better idea of the scope of research required by these courses, I have enclosed a copy of the introduction to and the bibliography for a paper I wrote entitled "The Effect of Hierarchical Organization on Intelligence Agencies: The Decision to Support the Invasion of Cuba." For other projects, I traveled to Washington, D.C., where I visited foreign embassies and international organizations and interviewed executives of American and foreign businesses.

Both of my internships (summer at the National Journalism Center and my senior year at a consulting firm specializing in international business) required extensive research and writing, but there I concentrated on economic and business questions rather than on the issues of foreign policy studied in college. At the National Journalism Center, I contributed to a series of articles on airline deregulation published in *The Tribune*. At the consulting firm, I concentrated on the implications for U.S. business of the emergence of the European Economic Community. I also drafted and edited articles for the firm's client newsletter on new federal legislation on commerce and trade.

Finally, I would mention that I was for three years a member of the Women's Caucus. As the organization's vice-president during my senior year, I organized and led a campaign to secure university funding for on-campus child care for the families of university employees. This facility now provides full-time child care for twenty children.

Personal Statement 3—Draft Version

Please provide any additional information that you would like to bring to the attention of the admissions committee.

I believe that I am a strong candidate for admission to business school because I have the ability to successfully complete my goals within a specific target date despite having to overcome tremendous obstacles and overwhelming odds in favor of my failure.

I came to the United States from Colombia, South America when I was only fourteen years old and that was the first time that I ever left my country or the company of my parents. I found myself scared, homesick, and lost in a foreign country. However, because I came to learn English, to receive an exceptional education, and to obtain better opportunities, I learned to overcome both cultural and language barriers and to approach life with an appreciation for hard work and the achievement of excellence.

My determination to meet my goals and my perseverance can best be demonstrated by my enormous academic improvement after my first semester of undergraduate college studies. During the first semester of my undergraduate studies, I received the lowest grades of my college career. My proficiency and understanding of the English language was insufficient to grasp the complexities of college level course work. However, after dedicating hundreds of hours to intensively studying and perfecting my English, the following semester I was able to obtain a 3.0 grade point average (out of a 4.0 scale). I was so successful in my efforts that I achieved excellent grades throughout the rest of my college studies, made the dean's list, received the minority Undergraduate Student of Excellence Award from the American Psychological Association and the university's psychology department, and graduated with Cum Laude honors.

Through my participation in extracurricular activities, I have cultivated strong analytical, communication, and leadership skills. First, I participated for two years in the "Faces of Diversity Committee." The Committee was composed of nine faculty members and one student. I was chosen for two consecutive years by the members of the committee to represent the student body.

The organization's objective was to increase awareness and dialogue among students regarding matters ranging from racial discrimination in the United States to customs and cultural differences of other countries. I accomplished this objective by arranging debates featuring panels of qualified professionals who would intelligently discuss with students these complex issues. My role during these debates was to serve as a moderator between the panelists and students with the two goals of stimulating meaningful dialogue between the two groups and managing an orderly development of the debates. My dedication, hard work, and responsibility towards accurately and meaningfully discussing these issues was exemplified by the increase in the number of students who attended these functions and by the same students' participation in the debates and their manifestation of greater awareness and acceptance of diverse cultures and individuals.

Furthermore, I was president of the International Students Organization, Vice President of the Latin American Students Association, and participation as an officer in many other campus organizations and community activities. I was elected president of the International Students Organization by 137 foreign students from 67 countries throughout the world to represent them before the university administration, student body assemblies, and International Student Organization sponsored functions. At the end of my term as president, I was given the Presidential Students Outstanding Award. The award is given by the university to only two students per year and it is the highest award that a student could ever receive from the university.

As Vice President of the Latin American Students Association, I organized festivals and cultural presentations with the goal of sharing our Hispanic culture with the university and the community.

Additionally, through working for several years as an international sales assistant at an international export company, I have developed the comparable skills and responsibility needed to successfully earn a business degree. I have a tremendous amount of knowledge of the environment and a wealth of experience in negotiating international business transactions.

As a sales assistant, I am responsible for our company's direct sales of multimillion dollar food processing equipment to our Latin American customers. My primary responsibility is to structure all of our equipment sales as documentary irrevocable letter of credit transactions. As a consequence of my employment, I have to study and thoroughly understand many aspects of the Uniform Commercial Code and the International Chamber of Commerce Publication No. 290. Likewise, I am responsible for drafting and negotiating sales contracts and reports to our Latin American customers, in both English and Spanish, outlining our company's position regarding letters of credit, bills of lading, banking arrangements, ocean freight arrangements, and other trade and customs issues.

Two other work experiences as a student Resident Advisor and as an inpatient clinical psychological counselor at a large city hospital will help me demonstrate abilities necessary to the successful completion of an M.B.A. These experiences have taught me how to competently function in stressful situations and effectively deal with individuals. As a resident advisor, I was responsible for the academic, physical, and emotional well-being of sixty female students. On many occasions I had to keenly deal with emergencies such as suicidal students, family crises, and criminal activities ranging from date rape to drug abuse. As a psychological counselor, I assisted in the treatment and studies of patients with mental disorders.

Overall, I believe that I have the ability and motivation to perform successfully in your business program and as a manager. Furthermore, I ask that you recognize that I worked a minimum of 30 hours per week throughout my college career. I maintained a 3.2 GPA, graduated Cum Laude, received many awards and scholarships for my academic performance, and am employed at an international export company as the youngest international sales assistant in charge of millions of dollars in sales throughout Latin America.

I would like to add that I am sure that I will meet many interesting people in business school, and I hope that they would find something interesting about me. My parents, Colombian citizens, are both practicing attorneys in Colombia; and as a child, I had the opportunity to learn much about the Roman Civil Legal System. I am fluent in Spanish as well as French and Portuguese. I have also studied dance for three years and concert flute for two years. As a child in Colombia, I performed with the Colombian National Academy of Andean Folkloric Dance.

CRITIQUE

This application is overflowing with the additional "plusses" that admissions officers are looking for—fluency in Spanish, English, French, and Portuguese and performances as a child with the Colombian National Academy of Andean Folkloric Dance! The candidate's GPA is a bit low for the target schools, but that is not likely to be a problem given the "qualitative measures" of the candidate's academic performance such as the Excellence Award.

Still, the personal statement can be considerably improved. The central organizing principle of the statement seems to be chronological; that can stay in place. It has a certain persuasiveness to it: I came to the United States; I studied hard to learn English; I started college and did not do all that well at first; I improved dramatically; I graduated with honors; I went to work; and I have done very well professionally. Some other organizational principle might have been chosen, but this development will do.

Setting aside some minor points (such as several split infinitives), the primary criticism is that the statement is much too long. Some minor points, such as the mention of the study of concert flute, need to be excised. Additionally, some points are repeated without reason. And a few points that are already contained in the Personal Data part of the application are mentioned without further elaboration and so should be deleted. Finally, in general, the wording of the discussion needs to be tightened up.

Personal Statement 3—Final Version

Please provide any additional information that you would like to bring to the attention of the admissions committee.

I came to the United States from Colombia, South America, to study English and to pursue my education. As a young woman, I found myself scared, homesick, and lost in a foreign country, but I did not give up. During the first semester of my undergraduate studies, I received the lowest grades of my college career. My understanding of English was at first insufficient to grasp the complexities of college-level courses. However, after spending many hours studying English, I obtained a 3.0 GPA my second semester. Later, in addition to graduating cum laude, I received the American Psychological Association's award for Minority Undergraduate Student Excellence (in conjunction with the university's psychology department). I attained these academic accomplishments while working a minimum of thirty hours per week throughout my college career.

Through my participation in extracurricular activities, I developed communication and leadership skills. For two years, I was chosen by the faculty members of the "Faces of Diversity Committee" as the student body's representative and moderated discussion panels on a variety of topics such as racial discrimination in the United States and cultural diversity. One hundred and thirty-seven students from sixty-seven different countries elected me president of the International Students organization for an unprecedented two consecutive years; and at the end of those terms, I received the Presidential Students Outstanding Award, the highest award that a student could ever receive from the university.

After graduating from college, I worked as a Resident Advisor and had responsibility for the academic, physical, and emotional well-being of sixty female students. On many occasions I had to deal with problems such as suicidal students, incidents of date rape, family crises, and drug abuse. Later, I worked as an inpatient psychological counselor at a large city hospital, assisting in the treatment and study of patients with mental disorders.

For the past several years, I have been working as an international sales assistant at an international export company. I am responsible for our company's multimillion-dollar direct sales of food-processing equipment to Latin American customers. My primary responsibility is to structure deals for equipment sales. I negotiate all aspects of the deals, including arranging for letters of credit, bills of lading, bank guarantees, and ocean freight as well as handling other trade and customs issues. As a consequence of my employment, I have to study and thoroughly understand the Uniform Commercial Code and the International Chamber of Commerce's Publication No. 290. I prepare these and other documents, such as our customer newsletter, in both English and Spanish.

Finally, I would like to add that I am sure that I will meet many interesting people in business school, and I hope that they will find something interesting about me. My parents, Colombian citizens, are both practicing attorneys in Colombia. I am fluent in French and Portuguese as well as Spanish and English. I studied dance for several years, and as a child I even performed with the Colombian National Academy of Andean Folkloric Dance.

Personal Statement 4—Draft Version

What personal skills and characteristics do you believe are most valuable in business? Which of them do you already have and how have you demonstrated that you have them? How will your study at the Graduate School of Business advance your career in business?

What business most values today is the effective manager. To be this, one must first manage himself, then manage others by his leadership. The highest priorities of an effective manager are to lead, develop, and build. They are accomplished using hard work, enthusiasm, perseverance, initiative, self-discipline, self-confidence, aggressiveness, positive thinking, empathy, efficiency, responsibility, courageousness, sound judgment, analytical ability, and honesty. An effective manager is a good coordinator, arbitrator, listener, decision maker, planner, motivator, communicator, administrator, innovator, salesman, and risk taker. A good manager must have an inquiring mind that constantly strives for excellence by seeking better ways of doing things. A good manager must not only be a problem solver but a problem preventer. A good manager must be goal oriented and visionary in seeing the end result, and implementing plans to achieve them. A good manager must be quick to praise and encourage others to help them achieve their maximum potential. Above all, business wants someone that will contribute more than their salary, and is a doer with the ability to make things happen to make money for the company.

I possess all of these characteristics in varying degrees and I am constantly improving both my strengths and weaknesses. Examples of how I have demonstrated I possess these are:

While with ABC International, a Salem-based manufacturer of shopping carts, I (1) acquired the most new customers during my first six months with the company, (2) redesigned dimensions of wheelchair shopping cart to conform to the various wheelchairs, thereby eliminating complaints and increasing goodwill, (3) overcame severe market resistance by marketing products ethically and with integrity, turning around customers' prior attitudes towards the company, (4) redesigned product brochures, resulting in more effective marketing at a lower cost, and (5) composed a direct mail marketing campaign which resulted in more effective acquisition of new customers.

While with XYZ Corporation, a Florida-based manufacturer of building products, I (1) motivated independent wholesaler salesmen to achieve maximum market penetration—one of the men I worked with earned a $2,000 company-sponsored vacation, while competing with others in Georgia, South Carolina, and Tennessee, (2) was cited by top management as an example of creative ideas and of always meeting deadlines, (3) was cited by more than one customer as "the best marketing representative that calls on us," (4) composed innovative marketing programs combining the use of co-op advertising, salesmen incentives, dating, and point of purchase displays, (5) increased sales from $1 million to $1.8 million despite discontinuance of two major products, (6) virtually eliminated other manufacturers of prefinished trim, most notably the Griffin division of U.S. Construction from my market area by acquiring over one hundred new retail outlets, (7) increased market penetration to over the region and the company average while decreasing market share of Building Goods, Inc., a major competitor, and (8) solved delicate distribution conflicts by combining policies of two-step distribution—selling independent dealers through wholesalers—and one-step distribution—selling national accounts and mass merchandisers direct.

By attending the Graduate Business School, I will acquire the additional business knowledge for myself that will enable me to fully utilize my knowledge for myself and contribute more effectively to the enterprise I am associated with. For example, this spring, I investigated going into business with a start-up company that had begun manufacturing a new type of drill bit. They needed a vice president of marketing to achieve market penetration in the hardware and home center industry selling through manufacturer's representatives. This position would have required an investment on my part. A graduate degree would have helped me formulate a business plan and analytically choose the best way to finance a business start-up, market most effectively, and judge chances for success before entering into the venture.

My planned course of emphasis in graduate school is on finance and marketing. My immediate goal is to achieve a wide variety of success in selling building materials through my present company. My next goal (three to five years) is to move into marketing management. After this, my goal is a general management function (seven to ten years) with responsibility for marketing, finance, and manufacturing. My ultimate goal is to head a division of a company in the building products industry that carries responsibility for profit and loss. I want to become a marketing management expert and would like to own my own business.

CRITIQUE

The prompt to which this statement is a response is one used by one of the most competitive business schools in the country, and many people reading the statement will probably think, "This person is obviously well qualified and articulate, and this is a really good answer to the question." This reaction is not completely unjustified; for the realm of top business schools, however, this is a statement that could benefit from considerably more work. It's not that the applicant is not qualified for this school; rather, this answer lacks imagination. Look at the part of the personal statement that responds to the question about what skills and characteristics are needed to succeed in business: hard work, enthusiasm, perseverance, initiative, self-discipline, etc. This is the same laundry list of adjectives with positive connotations that we hear when we watch interviews of professional athletes:

Interviewer: And what advice would you give to aspiring professional baseball players?

Athlete: You need to work hard, play with enthusiasm, persevere, and show the coaches that you have initiative and self-discipline.

Truly a formula for success in any endeavor! Now, this is not to say that these are not qualities that successful professionals—both managers and athletes—need; rather it is to say that in order to stand out, a personal statement needs to say something different.

In this statement, the lists of enumerated accomplishments that are supposed to demonstrate that this applicant has those characteristics don't match in any meaningful way the list of characteristics. To be sure, the list of characteristics is edifying, and the lists of accomplishments are impressive; but it is not clear how "redesigned product brochures" is connected to "enthusiasm" or how "motivated independent wholesaler salesmen" is connected with "sound judgment."

The paragraph regarding the opportunity to join a startup business doesn't really have much impact. The difficulty with it is that it describes a non-event: this did not happen. The final paragraph, however, is very good. This is the sort of concrete response that an admissions officer will be looking for.

Personal Statement 4—Final Version

What personal skills and characteristics do you believe are most valuable in business? Which of them do you already have and how have you demonstrated that you have them? How will your study at the Graduate School of Business advance your career in business?

Most of my business experience has been in sales, both as a sales representative having direct contact with customers and as a manager of other sales representatives. To be truly successful, a sales representative must be aggressive, innovative, understanding, and honest. Aggressiveness is, of course, the quality that people most often associate with sales, but a successful sales representative is not aggressive toward the customer (like the stereotypical, high-pressure salesman of cartoons) but toward the competition. While with ABC International, a manufacturer of shopping carts, I set a new company record for the number of new customers acquired during my first six months with the company. A successful sales representative must also be innovative. I redesigned ABC's product brochures, thereby creating a more effective marketing tool at a lower cost; and I devised a new direct-mail marketing campaign, which resulted in more effective acquisition of new customers. Understanding the customer's needs is also important. I redesigned the dimensions of our wheelchair shopping cart to be compatible with virtually all wheelchairs, thereby eliminating user complaints and boosting customer satisfaction. Finally, a successful sales representative must be honest. My predecessor at ABC International had used an array of questionable sales techniques, including misrepresentations about unit quality and delivery dates. By marketing products ethically, I was able to overcome severe market resistance due to customers' prior attitudes towards the company.

In addition to having the heart of a sales representative, a sales manager must know how to motivate the sales force, how to direct their efforts, and how to coordinate their efforts with the other activities of the company. While with XYZ Corporation, a manufacturer of building products, gross revenues generated by the sales force under my direction increased from $1 million to $1.8 million—in spite of the fact that during the same period the company discontinued two major products. This dramatic increase in sales virtually eliminated from the market other manufacturers of prefinished trim, most notably the powerful Griffin division of U.S. Construction. Additionally, a sales manager must know how to coordinate effort. At XYZ, I solved a delicate distribution conflict by combining a system of two-step distribution (selling to independent dealers through wholesalers) and one-step distribution (selling to national accounts and mass merchandisers directly). Finally, a sales manager must also coordinate the efforts of the sales force with the efforts of others within the company, and it is a point of pride that top management says about me, "He always meets deadlines."

The list of skills and characteristics that are needed for success in sales does not, however, include knowledge of financial planning, and that is my reason for going to business school. My planned course of emphasis in graduate school is on finance and marketing. My immediate goal is to achieve a high level of success marketing a wide variety of building materials through my present company. My next goal (three to five years) is to move into marketing management. After this, my goal is a general management function (seven to ten years) with responsibility for marketing, finance, and manufacturing. My ultimate goal is to head a division of a company in the building-products industry that carries responsibility for profit and loss.

Personal Statement 5—Draft Version

We are interested in what you are like as a person. Please describe some of your nonprofessional and/or nonacademic interests.

My interests are wide and diverse. My primary love is my wife, Paula, and my ten-year-old daughter, Beverly. I also love to read. I enjoy music, especially classical works and play the violin, having studied this instrument for more than ten years and attended Brookdale Arts Academy. I was concertmaster of my high school orchestra and am a member of three community orchestras. From this I learned discipline, how effective music can be in communication, and a great sense of accomplishment. I like being with people in social gatherings, exchanging ideas, and learning about them. I am constantly seeking out opportunities to meet new people as this helps me develop my social skills. I enjoy remodeling houses that I have owned because this gives me physical exercise and allows me to use my creative abilities. I enjoy bicycle rides with my family, sailboating, wind surfing, golf, and racquetball. I enjoy the exercise, the competitiveness, and becoming more accomplished at these sports.

CRITIQUE

This prompt is obviously intended to get at the "uniqueness" factor. You should recall that in chapter 2 the uniqueness factor was identified as being "something extra." The primary criticism of this response is that it is overkill. Assuming that the personal-statement responses to other prompts in the application have clearly established that the applicant has ability and motivation, there is no need to revisit those ideas in this response. If anything, the response to this prompt should be an understatement.

Personal Statement 5—Final Version

We are interested in what you are like as a person. Please describe some of your nonprofessional and/or nonacademic interests.

My primary love is my wife, Paula, and our ten-year-old daughter, Beverly. I enjoy bicycle rides with the family, sailboating, wind surfing, golf, and racquetball. I also enjoy music, especially classical music, and play the violin. I am a member of three community orchestras.

I also enjoy doing home repair and remodeling projects. It has always struck me as curious that many people regard this type of work as a tedious chore to be avoided or as beyond their ability and to be handed over to the local plumber or carpenter. While I would not want it to be my life's work, there is a great deal of self-satisfaction to be derived from "sweating" a length of copper tubing and seeing that the joint doesn't leak or building a new play area and watching kids have fun.

TAKING THE GMAT

As you learned in chapter 2, the GMAT is one of the two most important factors in your application (along with your GPA). This chapter focuses on the actual content of the GMAT, with sample problems to give you a sense of what the test is really like.

FORMAT

The GMAT consists of several (usually seven) separately timed sections containing multiple-choice questions, which are allotted twenty-five to thirty minutes apiece, plus one or two essay questions, which must also be completed within specified time limits. The essay questions must be written on assigned topics, though you will not know those topics in advance. The multiple-choice part of the test includes three math sections, three verbal sections, and one section that contains trial questions that are being tested for use on future versions of the GMAT. You will not, however, be told which are the trial questions, and you probably won't be able to identify them on your own.

SCORING

The test produces four different scores: an overall or composite score based on the multiple-choice questions, a quantitative subscore based just on the math questions, a verbal score based just on the multiple-choice reading, grammar, and logic questions, and an analytical writing assessment (AWA) score based on your essays. The composite score ranges from 200 (the minimum) to 800 (the maximum). The quantitative and verbal subscores range from 0 (the minimum) to 60 (the maximum). And the AWA score ranges from 0 (the minimum) to 6 (the maximum).

The multiple-choice parts of the test are scored using a formula that awards one point for each correct response and deducts one-quarter of a point for each incorrect response. This result is called the "raw" score. This raw score is then converted to a "scaled" score (from 200 to 800) using a scoring table that is unique to each particular form of the exam. For example, if on a 100-question test a candidate responds to 80 questions, getting 60 right and 20 wrong, the candidate's raw score would be:

$$60 - \left(\tfrac{1}{4}\right)(20) = 55$$

This result would then be converted to the 200-to-800-point scale using a table created by the test developers.

Your essay responses to the AWA prompts are read by two graders and assigned a score on the 0-to-6 scale. These scores are then averaged. To ensure that the grading is fair, if the two scores are more than a point apart, the essay is referred to a third grader who serves, in a way, as an arbiter.

GENERAL TEST-TAKING SUGGESTIONS
Guessing

The scoring formula for the multiple-choice parts of the test naturally raises the question of whether or not you should guess if you are not certain about the answer to an item. A good way of thinking about this issue is to analyze it using some concrete numbers. Let us assume that a candidate guesses on twenty items. Since there are five answer choices for each item, the chance of answering correctly is one out of five, so (theoretically at least) the candidate should answer correctly on:

$$\tfrac{1}{5} \times 20 = 4$$

And that means sixteen missed questions for a deduction of:

$$\tfrac{1}{4} \times 16 = 4$$

For a net score of:

$$4 - 4 = 0$$

In other words, no harm, no foul.

Of course, on a lucky day you might show a net gain from random guessing, but on an unlucky day you might show a net loss. The best strategy, therefore, is to omit any item that you have absolutely no idea how to answer. On the other hand, if you are able to eliminate one or more choices as incorrect, then it is to your advantage to choose one of the remaining options. Again, let's work with some numbers. Let us make the admittedly unrealistic assumption that a candidate is able to eliminate exactly one choice on each of twenty items. What would be the result of choosing randomly from among the four remaining options on each item? Since the chance of answering correctly is now one out of four, the number of correct answers should be:

$$\tfrac{1}{4} \times 20 = 5$$

And that means fifteen incorrect items for a deduction of:

$$\tfrac{1}{4} \times 15 = 3\tfrac{3}{4}$$

For a net of:

$$5 - 3\tfrac{3}{4} = 1\tfrac{1}{4}$$

Which will be rounded down to one—but that's still a net gain of one.

The general rule, then, is that simply guessing blindly is not likely to improve your score and could very well hurt your performance. On the other hand, educated guessing—when you are able to eliminate one or more choices as incorrect—is a valuable test-taking tactic.

The Answer Document

Your answers to the multiple-choice sections of the test are indicated by darkening numbered ovals on a separate answer document. This answer document is then read by a scanning machine, and your score is calculated by computer. Obviously, then, you want to make sure that you code your responses in a way that ensures that the machine will read your answer document accurately:

- Use a No. 2 (soft lead) pencil.
- Darken the oval completely.
- Darken only one oval per item.
- Erase all stray marks completely and thoroughly.
- Place your answers in the proper locations.

Also, you may find that your answer document contains more numbered spaces for answers than there are questions in your test booklet. Simply leave those blank.

The last point in the list above deserves special consideration. The scanning machine that grades the tests can read only what is on the paper it scans—it cannot read the intentions of the person who penciled in those ovals. In this respect, the scoring system is absolutely unforgiving of coding errors. That is, if you solve a problem correctly but darken the wrong oval on the answer document, the scanning machine reads that mark as an incorrect response. Not only do you not get the point for a correct answer, you get a deduction of one-quarter point. This can be devastating when an entire sequence of responses is misplaced, as might occur if you intend to leave a question blank because you are unable to solve it but fail to skip the corresponding space on the answer sheet. The correct sequence is displaced up one row, and the result is equivalent to random guessing: The chance that the response intended for one item will also be the correct response to the item immediately above it is just one out of five.

A good technique for avoiding this problem is to code your answers in groups. Instead of working an item and then pulling out your answer document to code your response, work a small group of items—perhaps even an entire page—keeping track of your responses by circling the correct choice in the test booklet (or some similar method). Then, when you have finished a group, code your responses on the answer sheet. This will help to ensure that you don't make a mistake, and this method is more efficient than shuffling papers after each question.

Directions

The registration bulletin for the GMAT advises:

> During the test administration, read all directions carefully.

In fact, this is very bad advice. The format of the GMAT is announced in advance in the registration bulletin that is revised annually by the test's sponsor, and the directions for each different type of question are provided. By reading the directions in advance and becoming familiar with the types of questions used, you will be able to recognize each type just by its format and will know what is expected without having to read directions. The time you save may allow you to answer several more questions and achieve a higher score.

SAMPLE QUESTIONS

You can use the practice answer document below to mark your answers to the multiple-choice questions that follow. The answer documents for the analytical writing prompts allow for writing on three sides of $8\frac{1}{2} \times 11$ (letter-size) paper.

SECTION 1	SECTION 2	SECTION 3	SECTION 4	SECTION 5
1 Ⓐ Ⓑ Ⓒ Ⓓ Ⓔ	7 Ⓐ Ⓑ Ⓒ Ⓓ Ⓔ	13 Ⓐ Ⓑ Ⓒ Ⓓ Ⓔ	19 Ⓐ Ⓑ Ⓒ Ⓓ Ⓔ	25 Ⓐ Ⓑ Ⓒ Ⓓ Ⓔ
2 Ⓐ Ⓑ Ⓒ Ⓓ Ⓔ	8 Ⓐ Ⓑ Ⓒ Ⓓ Ⓔ	14 Ⓐ Ⓑ Ⓒ Ⓓ Ⓔ	20 Ⓐ Ⓑ Ⓒ Ⓓ Ⓔ	26 Ⓐ Ⓑ Ⓒ Ⓓ Ⓔ
3 Ⓐ Ⓑ Ⓒ Ⓓ Ⓔ	9 Ⓐ Ⓑ Ⓒ Ⓓ Ⓔ	15 Ⓐ Ⓑ Ⓒ Ⓓ Ⓔ	21 Ⓐ Ⓑ Ⓒ Ⓓ Ⓔ	27 Ⓐ Ⓑ Ⓒ Ⓓ Ⓔ
4 Ⓐ Ⓑ Ⓒ Ⓓ Ⓔ	10 Ⓐ Ⓑ Ⓒ Ⓓ Ⓔ	16 Ⓐ Ⓑ Ⓒ Ⓓ Ⓔ	22 Ⓐ Ⓑ Ⓒ Ⓓ Ⓔ	28 Ⓐ Ⓑ Ⓒ Ⓓ Ⓔ
5 Ⓐ Ⓑ Ⓒ Ⓓ Ⓔ	11 Ⓐ Ⓑ Ⓒ Ⓓ Ⓔ	17 Ⓐ Ⓑ Ⓒ Ⓓ Ⓔ	23 Ⓐ Ⓑ Ⓒ Ⓓ Ⓔ	29 Ⓐ Ⓑ Ⓒ Ⓓ Ⓔ
6 Ⓐ Ⓑ Ⓒ Ⓓ Ⓔ	12 Ⓐ Ⓑ Ⓒ Ⓓ Ⓔ	18 Ⓐ Ⓑ Ⓒ Ⓓ Ⓔ	24 Ⓐ Ⓑ Ⓒ Ⓓ Ⓔ	30 Ⓐ Ⓑ Ⓒ Ⓓ Ⓔ

Reading Comprehension

The Reading Comprehension section of the GMAT consists of several passages, up to 550 words long, which discuss business-related topics as well as topics from the social, physical, and biological sciences. Each passage is followed by questions that ask you to interpret, apply, or draw inferences from the information in the reading. The GMAT includes eighteen to twenty-three reading comprehension questions.

<u>Directions:</u> **The passage below is followed by questions based on its content. After reading the passage, choose the best answer to each question and fill in the corresponding oval on your answer sheet. Answer the questions on the basis of what is *stated* or *implied* in the passage.**

The spread of Christianity to Africa may be regarded as the religious aspect of Western expansion. European missionaries naturally favored the aims of their respective countries, even as they viewed the extension of Western hegemony as redemptive, insofar as it brought Africans freedom from oppression, anarchy, and the slave trade. The glory of God and the glory of country were intertwined in the mission thought, and many missionaries saw salvation for Africa in terms of Western civilization, of which Christianity was an integral element. To the missionary, the spirit of the Christian God was history's engine; but so closely tied to specific national interests was this belief that when Catholics and Protestants competed for the same African souls, as in Uganda, it left deep social cleavages. Converts to Catholicism became known as "bafransa," after the nationality (French) of the missionaries, while Anglicans were referred to as "baingereza," the Ganda word for the English. So deep was this division that political loyalties subsequently followed the same division, a legacy that has inhibited the unification of the country to this day.

The task of bringing Western "civilization" to Africa encountered great difficulty because of what were from the standpoint of African thinking inherent contradictions: on the one hand, its secular technique is based on profound materialism; on the other, its dominant religion, Christianity, embodies values that are irreconcilable with materialism. Westerners deal with this contradiction by relegating religious experience to a separate realm, but this metaphysical discontinuity cannot be translated into African terms. In Africa, the dichotomy between ethics and behavior, between religious and social life, is unknown.

Even to those who benefited from mission school education, Christianity had only limited appeal. By insisting on a theology and a liturgy that made little sense to thoughtful Africans, the church failed to inspire the loyalty of many of those whom it had educated. Contact with the church became merely convenient—a means of enhancing one's own career prospects outside of rather than inside the institution. It is no coincidence that Kwame Nkrumah, the first president of Ghana and one of the vanguard of the Pan-African movement, advised fellow nationalist leaders to "seek first the political kingdom, and everything else will be added." When nationalist leaders like Nkrumah portrayed themselves as political messiahs, they engaged in a counteroffensive inspired by the indigenous notion that the religious and the secular are one; and in order to dismantle colonialism, it was natural to insist on politics as supreme and hegemonic and to demand the subordination of any ideology other than that embraced by the new nationalist leadership.

Although most church leaders believed that they had no option but to follow the commands of the new political leadership, the Africanization of the church leadership encouraged the first real search for African Christianity. The objectives were to identify an African element in the field of theology and religious activities that could keep pace with the ideological strides toward greater political and cultural autonomy.

Today, a growing number of African theologians are engaged in precisely this task, often extending it to include the role of the society. Many Africans, however, broke away from the mission churches and started their own religious movements. In some instances, African prophets wishing to merge the Christian message with their own religious praxis were excommunicated and forced to start their own sects. As in the division and multiplication of Protestant churches in Europe in the 17th, 18th, and 19th centuries, these organizations proved particularly successful among the poor and illiterate strata of the African population. The messianic leaders of these African sects, basing their theology on the indigenous notion that there is no such thing as a disembodied soul, significantly limited the expansion of the mission church among ordinary Africans.

1. Which of the following best summarizes the main point of the passage?

   (A) The attempt to develop an African Christianity is complicated by both the political legacy of Western expansion and Christian theology.

   (B) Christian missionaries hoped to advance the political aims of their respective countries as well as to spread their religion.

   (C) Christianity has often been used as a political tool to help subjugate colonized people by teaching them a passive mentality.

   (D) Western Christianity can never flourish in Africa because Christian doctrines cannot be translated into the African world view.

   (E) The influence of Christianity in Africa is found primarily in the messianic cults that attract the poor and illiterate.

2. According to the passage, Western ideas were not embraced by Africans because:

   (A) Christian missionaries were overly concerned with advancing the political aims of their own countries

   (B) early advocates of the Pan-African movement insisted that politics take precedence over religion

   (C) the distinction between politics as worldly and religion as otherworldly is alien to Africa

    (D) missionaries from different countries preached contradictory Christian doctrines

    (E) the mission church failed to educate the poor and illiterate strata of the African population

3. It can be inferred that some African religious leaders were excommunicated from the mission church because they:

    (A) refused to accept the church's teaching regarding the body-soul dichotomy

    (B) wanted to dismantle the structure of Western colonialism

    (C) argued that it is impossible to reconcile Christian doctrine with Western materialism

    (D) proclaimed that politics is the supreme ideology and nationalism its God

    (E) deluded the uneducated masses into thinking that their teachings were truly Christian

4. The author mentions the "bafransa" and "baingereza" in order to:

    (A) demonstrate that the Christian distinction between religion and politics is not distinctly African

    (B) illustrate the lasting effects of the political overtones of Christian missionary efforts

    (C) cast doubt on the possibility of reconciling Christian theology with African concepts

    (D) draw a distinction between the religion of the educated African and that of the illiterate African

    (E) preempt a possible objection to the claim that Christian missionaries visited Africa

5. Which of the following would be the most appropriate topic for the author to pursue in a paragraph following the last paragraph of the passage?

    (A) Trace the history of the development of the Christian notion of a disembodied soul.

    (B) Provide further details of the attempts of the mission church to convert Africans.

    (C) Analyze the effects of the Pan-African movement on colonial structures.

(D) Elaborate on the rise and expansion of Protestant sects in the 17th, 18th, and 19th centuries.

(E) Describe attempts by contemporary theologians to reconcile Christian teachings with African concepts.

6. The author's treatment of the topic can best be described as:

(A) scholarly yet sympathetic

(B) scientific yet amused

(C) balanced yet impassioned

(D) caustic and biased

(E) casual and superficial

Critical Reasoning

The Critical Reasoning section consists of an argument or set of statements followed by one to three questions about the information given. The questions are designed to test the reasoning skills required to construct and evaluate arguments and to formulate and evaluate a plan of action. The GMAT includes sixteen critical-reasoning questions.

Directions: In this section, the questions ask you to analyze and evaluate the reasoning presented in a statement or short paragraph. For some questions, all of the choices may arguably be answers to the question asked, but you are to select the best answer to the question. In evaluating the choices to a question, do not make assumptions that violate common-sense standards by being implausible, redundant, irrelevant, or inconsistent. After you have chosen the best answer, fill in the corresponding oval on your answer sheet.

7. There is something irrational about our system of laws. The criminal law punishes a person who attempts to commit a crime even though the crime is never actually committed. But under the civil law a person who attempts to defraud a victim and is unsuccessful is not required to pay damages.

Which of the following, if true, would most weaken the argument above?

(A) Most persons who are imprisoned for crimes will commit another crime if they are ever released from prison.

(B) A person is morally culpable for evil thoughts as well as for evil deeds.

(C) There are more criminal laws on the books than there are civil laws.

(D) A criminal trial is considerably more costly to the state than a civil trial.

(E) The goal of the criminal law is to punish the criminal, but the goal of the civil law is to compensate the victim.

8. A new restaurant will open soon on the corner of Bleecker Street and Seventh Avenue, and the owners have applied for a license to operate a sidewalk café. This application should be rejected. Pedestrian traffic on that corner is heavy, particularly on Friday and Saturday nights. Moreover, that stretch of sidewalk is narrow due to the angle of intersection of the streets. A sidewalk café would seriously obstruct pedestrian traffic, causing inconvenience and even creating a safety hazard as pedestrians are diverted into the street.

Which of the following best expresses the conclusion of the argument above?

(A) A new restaurant should not be permitted at the intersection.

(B) The new restaurant should not be permitted to operate a sidewalk café.

(C) A sidewalk café at the location of the new restaurant would pose a danger to pedestrians.

(D) Pedestrian traffic at the intersection is heaviest on Friday and Saturday nights.

(E) The angle at which the streets intersect makes the sidewalk narrow.

9. *John*: We learned in biology today that most mammals live on land.

Fred: That's not true. Just the other day the teacher said that whales are mammals that live in the sea.

Fred's remark shows that he has misunderstood John to say that:

(A) some mammals do not live on land

(B) no mammals live on land

(C) all mammals live on land

(D) all animals that live in the sea are mammals

(E) whales are not true mammals

10. Something must be done about the rising cost of our state prisons. It now costs an average of $225 per day to maintain a prisoner in a double-occupancy cell in a state prison. Yet, in the most expensive cities in the world, you can find rooms in good hotels that rent for less than $200 per night.

Which of the following, if true, would be the most serious objection to the argument?

(A) Many prisoners would prefer to be housed in single-occupancy rather than double-occupancy cells.

(B) The most expensive hotels in the world have rooms that cost more than $200 per night.

(C) The cost of maintaining a prison includes costs such as security and meals that hotels do not incur.

(D) Many prisons are not located in the center of large cities.

(E) A hotel guest is permitted to choose a hotel, while a prisoner is assigned to a particular institution.

11. At the beginning of 1990, the Town of Lake George imposed a "bed" tax on all hotel bills equal to 2 percent of the amount of the bill. The summer of 1990 was the worst year for tourism in Lake George in a decade. On January 1, 1991, the Town repealed the bed tax, and tourism for the summer of 1991 was up 20 percent over the previous year. We can see now what a devastating economic impact the bed tax had on the Lake George tourism industry.

Each of the following indicates a possible flaw in the reasoning in the passage above except:

(A) The nation was in a recession in 1990 but had recovered by the summer of 1991.

(B) From 1990 to 1991, hotels in Lake George reduced their room rates by an average of 15 percent.

(C) Over the first six months of 1991, the Lake George Commission on Tourism heavily advertised the community as a vacation spot.

(D) For Bolton Landing, the town next to Lake George with no bed tax in 1990, the summer of 1990 was the best for tourism in the town's history.

(E) Fun Park, a major tourist attraction in Lake George, was closed the entire summer of 1990 for renovation.

12. It is sometimes argued that we are reaching the limits of the earth's capacity to supply our energy needs with fossil fuel. In the past ten years, however, as a result of technological progress making it possible to extract resources from even marginal wells and mines, yields from oil and coal fields have increased tremendously. There is no reason to believe that there is a limit to the earth's capacity to supply our conventional energy needs.

Which of the following statements most directly contradicts the conclusion drawn above?

(A) Even if we exhaust our supplies of fossil fuel, the earth can still be mined for uranium.

(B) The technology needed to extract fossil fuels is very expensive.

(C) Even given the improvements in technology, oil and coal are not renewable resources, so we will exhaust our supplies.

(D) Most of the land under which marginal oil and coal supplies lie is more suitable to cultivation or pasturing than to production of fossil fuels.

(E) The fuels that are yielded by marginal sources tend to be high in sulphur and other undesirable elements that aggravate the air pollution problem.

Sentence Correction

The Sentence Correction section tests your ability to recognize correct (grammatically and structurally sound) and effective (clear and concise) expression. Sentence correction questions ask you to choose which of five choices best expresses a particular idea. The GMAT includes twenty-two sentence correction questions.

<u>Directions:</u> **In each of the following sentences, part or all of the sentence is underlined. Following each sentence are five different ways of wording the underlined part. Answer choice (A) always repeats the original; the other four choices are different. If you think that the sentence as originally written is the best way of wording the underlined part, choose answer (A); otherwise, select the best alternative. Fill in the corresponding oval on your answer sheet.**

This section tests your ability to identify correct and effective expression. Evaluate the answer choices by the requirements of standard written English. Pay attention to elements of grammar, diction (choice of words), and sentence construction. Select the answer choice that best renders the thought presented in the original sentence. The correct choices will be clear, and precise and free of awkwardness, needless repetition, or ambiguity.

13. It should be emphasized that, contrary to common opinion, undercapitalization, not management errors, <u>are the most important cause</u> of failure of small businesses.

   (A) are the most important cause

   (B) are the more important cause

   (C) is the most important cause

   (D) is the most important causes

   (E) is the more important cause

14. It was expected that the committee would recommend more stringent requirements for graduation, but its members <u>will make no formal report until they studied further the decline in test scores and their cause.</u>

   (A) will make no formal report until they studied further the decline in test scores and their cause

   (B) will make no formal report until it studied further the decline in test scores and their cause

   (C) will make no formal report until they have further studied the test scores, their declines and their causes

(D) will make no formal report until they have studied further the decline in test scores and its cause

(E) have made no formal report until they will study further the decline in test scores and its cause

15. The psychotherapist does not cure the patient by administering a treatment; they listen to the patient and invite the patient to treat himself or herself.

(A) they listen to the patient and invite

(B) he or she listens to the patient and invites

(C) he or she hears the patient and invites

(D) their listening to the patient invites

(E) by listening to the patient, they invite

16. Most pacifists oppose all forms of organized violence out of religious or philosophical commitment to the sanctity of human life.

(A) out of religious or philosophical commitment to the sanctity of human life

(B) by committing themselves religiously or philosophically to the sanctity of human life

(C) in that human life commands their religious or philosophical commitment

(D) in that they sanctify, religiously or philosophically, human life

(E) committing themselves to the sanctity of human life in their religion or philosophy

17. The review was very critical of the film, citing the poor photography, the weak plot, and that the dialogue was stilted.

(A) and that the dialogue was stilted

(B) and the dialogue was stilted

(C) while the dialogue was stilted

(D) and the stilted dialogue

(E) and also including the stilted dialogue

18. An objective reporter, Holmes has spared <u>neither criticism nor praise for</u> the Mayor's program.

   (A) neither criticism nor praise for

   (B) either criticism or praise for

   (C) neither criticism of nor praise for

   (D) either criticism of or praise for

   (E) both criticism of and praise for

Problem Solving

Questions in the Problem Solving section test your ability to understand and solve quantitative problems using arithmetic, elementary algebra, or commonly known geometry concepts. Questions are equally divided between strictly mathematical problems and "real-life" word problems. The GMAT includes thirty-two problem-solving questions divided into two sections.

Directions: Solve each of the following problems and indicate the best answer choice by filling in the appropriate oval on your answer sheet. You may use any available space for scratchwork.

Numbers: All values are real numbers.

Figures: A figure accompanying a problem in this section is intended to supply information that would be useful in solving the problem. The figures are drawn as accurately as possible unless the figure is accompanied by a note specifically stating that the particular figure is not drawn to scale. Unless otherwise indicated, all figures lie in a plane.

19. $(2,502)^2 - (2,500 \times 2,502) =$

   (A) 2   **(B)** 4   **(C)** 2,500

   (D) 5,000   **(E)** 5,004

20. For a certain year, a public utility reported earnings of $14.68 per share. The reported earnings per share for the fourth quarter were $4.42. If the number of shares did not change during the year, what were the average quarterly earnings for the first three quarters of the year?

(A) $3.42   (B) $3.67   (C) $5.62

(D) $6.84   (E) $10.25

21. If $7 - 2x = y + 2$, then $5 - 2xy =$

(A) $y + 1$ (B) $2y + 4$ (C) y

(D) $y - 2$ (E) $y - 4$

22. A merchant gives customers a 20 percent discount on the usual selling price of an item. If the merchant still realizes a net profit of 25 percent on the $16.00 cost of the item, what is the usual selling price of the item?

(A) $20.00   (B) $20.60   (C) $24.00

(D) $25.00   (E) $26.67

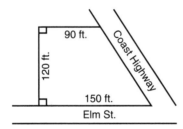

23. The figure above shows a piece of property with two street frontages. What is the area of the property in square feet?

(A) 7,200   (B) 10,800   (C) 14,400

(D) 18,800   (E) 24,000

24. The populations of County X and County Y both grew by 8 percent from 1980 to 1990. If the population of County X grew by 80,000 and the population of County Y grew by 84,000, what was the difference between the population of County X in 1990 and that of County Y in 1990?

(A) 58,000   (B) 54,000   (C) 50,000

(D) 46,000   (E) 40,000

Data Sufficiency

Problems in the Data Sufficiency section consist of a question followed by two statements, labeled (1) and (2), which contain additional information. You must decide whether the information contained in statement (1) or statement (2) alone or in the two statements taken together is sufficient to answer the question. The questions are intended to measure your ability to analyze a quantitative problem, to recognize relevant information, and to determine the point at which you have all the information you need to solve the problem. The GMAT includes twenty data sufficiency questions.

Directions: Each of the items below consists of a question followed by two statements, labeled (1) and (2). You must determine whether the information provided by the numbered statements is sufficient to answer the question asked. In addition to the information provided in the numbered statements, you should rely on your knowledge of mathematics and ordinary facts (such as the number of minutes in an hour). On your answer sheet, fill in oval

A if statement (1) BY ITSELF is sufficient to answer the question but statement (2) by itself is not sufficient to answer the question;

B if statement (2) BY ITSELF is sufficient to answer the question but statement (1) by itself is not sufficient to answer the question;

C if BOTH statements (1) and (2) TOGETHER are sufficient to answer the question but NEITHER statement BY ITSELF is sufficient to answer the question;

D if EACH statement BY ITSELF is sufficient to answer the question; and

E if the two statements, even when taken TOGETHER, are NOT sufficient to answer the question.

Numbers: All values are real numbers.

Figures: The figures in this section will not necessarily reflect the information given in the numbered statements, but they will reflect the information provided in the question.

Unless otherwise indicated, all figures lie in a plane; all lines shown as straight are straight; and the positions of all points, angles, regions, etc., are correctly depicted.

Example:

In ABC, what is the value of x?

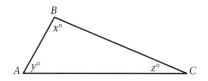

(1) $y = 60$

(2) $AB = BC$

Explanation: Statement (1) is not sufficient to answer the question, because statement (1) provides no information about x or z. Statement (2) is not sufficient to answer the question. Statement (2) does establish that $y = z$, but that is not enough information to determine the value of x. Both statements together are sufficient to answer the question. Since $AB = BC$ and $y = z$, $z = 60$. Since $x + y + z = 180$, $x = 60$.

25. What is the price of a single room for one night at the Hotel California?

   (1) The price of a single room for one night at the Hotel California is less than the $50 charged by the Dew Drop Inn but more than the $40 charged by the Notell Motel.

   (2) The price of a double room for one night at the Hotel California is $90, exactly twice the price of a single room.

26. This year the enrollment of a certain school is 5 percent higher than last year. What is this year's enrollment?

   (1) 180 students graduated last year.

   (2) There are 38 new transfer students who enrolled this year.

27. Is $x > y$?

   (1) $(x - y) > 0$

   (2) $x^2 > y^2$

28. If two polygons, S and T, are each equilateral and equiangular, is the perimeter of S longer than that of T?

(**1**) The degree measure of the angles of S is greater than that of T.

(**2**) The side of S is longer than the side of T.

29. If a certain pouch contains only coins currently minted by the U.S. Treasury, how many coins are in the pouch?

(**1**) The pouch contains exactly 44 cents.

(**2**) The pouch contains at least one quarter, at least one dime, at least one nickel, and at least one penny.

30. John and Phil each deposited exactly 50 cents per month into their respective piggy banks each month during a certain year, starting in January. If no withdrawals were made, which bank has more money in it at the end of the year?

(**1**) After the March deposit, John's bank contains exactly three times as much money as Phil's.

(**2**) After the June deposit, John's bank contains exactly twice as much money as Phil's.

Analytical Writing

The Analytical Writing Assessment consists of two thirty-minute writing tasks designed to test your reasoning and communication skills. One task requires you to analyze an issue, and the other to analyze an argument. For the analysis of an issue, you will be expected to take a position on a given issue and to explain the reasoning behind your point of view, citing examples from your reading or from personal experience. For the analysis of an argument, you will be required to explain the reasoning behind a given argument and to write a critique of the specific line of reasoning used to produce the specific conclusion offered. Both the issue and the argument concern topics of general interest and neither presupposes any specific knowledge of business or any other content area.

Directions: **Read the statement below and the directions. Write your response on lined $8\frac{1}{2} \times 11$ (letter-size) paper, using no more than three sides.**

Some people prefer formal gardens. They feel that the clean lines and orderly arrangements reflect a balanced and orderly view of life. Other people prefer informal gardens because they feel that they reflect the creativity and diversity of nature while formal gardens reflect a desire of humans to master nature.

Which view do you find more persuasive? Explain yhour position using relevant reasons and/or examples drawn from your own experience, observations, or reading.

Answer Key to Multiple-Choice Items

1. A	**7.** E	**13.** C	**19.** E	**25.** B
2. C	**8.** B	**14.** D	**20.** A	**26.** E
3. A	**9.** C	**15.** B	**21.** C	**27.** A
4. B	**10.** C	**16.** A	**22.** D	**28.** C
5. E	**11.** D	**17.** D	**23.** C	**29.** C
6. A	**12.** C	**18.** C	**24.** B	**30.** D

AACSB–Accredited Schools of Business

Alabama

Auburn University
College of Business
Auburn University, AL 36849
205 844–4030

Auburn University at Montgomery
School of Business
7300 University Drive
Montgomery, AL 36117
205 244–3476

University of Alabama
Manderson Graduate School of
  Business
P.O. Box 870223
Tuscaloosa, AL 35487–0223
205 348–7443

University of Alabama at
  Birmingham
School of Business
University Station
Birmingham, AL 35294
205 934–8810

University of South Alabama
College of Business &
  Management Studies
Mobile, AL 36688
205 460–6418

Alaska

University of Alaska Fairbanks
School of Management
Fairbanks, AK 99775
907 474–7878

ARIZONA

Arizona State University
College of Business
Tempe, AZ 85287–3506
602 965–5516

Northern Arizona University
College of Business Administration
Box 15066
Flagstaff, AZ 86011–5066
602 523–3657

University of Arizona
Karl Eller Graduate School of
  Management
Eller School, College of Business
  & Public Admin.
Tucson, AZ 85721
602 621–2165

ARKANSAS

Arkansas State University
College of Business
P.O. Box 1630
State University, AR 72467
501 972–3035

University of Arkansas
College of Business Administration
BADM 328
Fayetteville, AR 72701
501 575–4551

University of Arkansas at
  Little Rock
College of Business Administration
2801 South University Avenue
Little Rock, AR 72204
501 569–3356

University of Central Arkansas
College of Business Administration
Burdick #222
Conway, AR 72032
501 450–3106

CALIFORNIA

California Polytechnic State
  University, San Luis Obispo
School of Business
San Luis Obispo, CA 93407
805 756–2637

California State University,
  Bakersfield
School of Business & Public
  Administration
9001 Stockdale Highway
Bakersfield, CA 93311

California State University, Chico
College of Business
Chico, CA 95929
916 898–6271

California State University, Fresno
School of Business &
  Administrative Services
Fresno, CA 93740–0008
209 278–4240

California State University,
  Fullerton
School of Business Administration
  & Economics
800 N. State College Boulevard
Fullerton, CA 92634
714 773–2211

California State University,
Hayward
School of Business & Economics
Hayward, CA 94542
415 881–3311

California State University,
Long Beach
School of Business Administration
1250 Bellflower Boulevard
Long Beach, CA 90840
310 985–5306

California State University,
Los Angeles
School of Business and
Economics
5151 State University Drive
Los Angeles, CA 90032–8120
213 343–2800

California State University,
Northridge
School of Business Administration
& Economics
18111 Nordhoff Street
Northridge, CA 91330
818 885–2467

California State University,
Sacramento
School of Business & Public
Administration
6000 J Street
Sacramento, CA 95819
916 278–6011

Loyola Marymount University
College of Business Administration
7101 W. 80th Street
Los Angeles, CA 90045
213 338–2731

San Diego State University
College of Business Administration
San Diego, CA 92182
619 594–5200

San Francisco State University
Graduate School of Business
1600 Holloway Avenue
San Francisco, CA 94132
415 338–1276

San Jose State University
College of Business
One Washington Square
BT 250
San Jose, CA 95192–0162
408 924–3400

Santa Clara University
Leavey School of Business &
Administration
820 Alviso Street
Santa Clara, CA 95053
408 554–4500

Stanford University
Graduate School of Business
Stanford, CA 94305–5015
415 723–2146

University of California at
Berkeley
Walter A. Haas School of Business
350 Barrows Hall
Berkeley, CA 94720
501 642–6000

University of California at Irvine
Graduate School of Management
Campus Drive
Irvine, CA 92717

University of California,
  Los Angeles
John E. Anderson Graduate School
  of Management
405 Hilgard Avenue
Los Angeles, CA 90024–1481
213 825–6121

University of San Diego
School of Business
Alcala Park
San Diego, CA 92110
619 260–4830

University of San Francisco
McLaren Graduate School of
  Management
Ignatian Heights
2130 Fulton Street
San Francisco, CA 94117–1080
415 666–6771

University of Southern California
Graduate School of Business
  Administration
701 Exposition Boulevard
Hoffman Hall 800
Los Angeles, CA 90089–1421
213 740–0674

COLORADO

Colorado State University
College of Business
Fort Collins, CO 80523
303 491–6471

University of Colorado at Boulder
Graduate School of Business
  Administration
Campus Box #419
Boulder, CO 80309–0419
303 492–7124

University of Colorado at
  Colorado Springs
College of Business &
  Administration
P.O. Box 7150
1420 Austin Bluffs Parkway
Colorado Springs, CO 80933–7150
719 593–3408

University of Colorado at Denver
College of Business Administration
P.O. Box 173364
Denver, CO 80217–3364
303 628–1200

University of Denver
Graduate School of Business
  Administration
2020 S. Race #122
Denver, CO 80208
303 871–3416

CONNECTICUT

University of Bridgeport
College of Business & Public
  Management
126 Park Avenue
Bridgeport, CT 06601

University of Connecticut
School of Business Administration
368 Fairfield Road U-41D
Storrs, CT 06269–2041
203 486–2317

Yale University
School of Organization &
  Management
Box 1-A Yale Station
New Haven, CT 06520
203 432–5932

Delaware

University of Delaware
College of Business &
  Economics
Newark, DE 19716
302 451–1211

District of Columbia

The American University
Kogod College of Business
  Administration
4400 Massachusetts Avenue NW
Washington, DC 20016
202 885–1900

George Washington University
School of Business & Public
  Management
710 21st Street NW
Washington, DC 20052
202 994–8565

Georgetown University
School of Business Administration
105 Old North Building
Washington, DC 20057
202 687–4112

Howard University
School of Business
2600 Sixth Street, NW
Washington, DC 20059
202 806–5100

Florida

Florida Atlantic University
College of Business Administration
Business 219
Boca Raton, FL 33431
407 367–3982

Florida International University
College of Business Administration
University Park
Miami, FL 33199
305 348–2000

Florida State University
College of Business
Dean's Office, Room 314 RBA
Tallahassee, FL 32306–1042
904 644–3090

Rollins College
Roy E. Crummer Graduate School
  of Business
Winter Park, FL 32789
407 646–2540

University of Central Florida
College of Business Administration
Suite 230
Orlando, FL 32816–0991
407 823–2181

University of Florida
Graduate School of Business
301 Business Building
Gainesville, FL 32611
904 392–2397

University of Miami
School of Business Administration
P.O. Box 248027
219 Jenkins Building
Coral Gables, FL 33124–6520
305 284–4643

University of North Florida
College of Business Administration
4567 St. John's Bluff Road South
Jacksonville, FL 32216
904 646–2590

University of South Florida
College of Business Administration
4202 East Fowler Avenue
Tampa, FL 33620
813 974–4281

GEORGIA

Clark Atlanta University
School of Business Administration
James P. Brawley Drive at Fair
  Street
Atlanta, GA 30314
404 880–8000

Emory University
Emory Business School
1602 Mizell Drive
Atlanta, GA 30322
404 727–6270

Georgia Institute of Technology
College of Management
755 Ferst Drive
Atlanta, GA 30332
404 894–2600

Georgia Southern University
School of Business
Hwy 301
Landrum Box 8024
Statesboro, GA 30460
912 681–5767

Georgia State University
College of Business Administration
30 Pryor Street
Atlanta, GA 30303
404 651–2600

University of Georgia
Graduate School of Business
  Administration
351 Brooks Hall, GSB
Athens, GA 30602
404 542–5671

West Georgia College
College of Business
1600 Maple Street
Carrollton, GA 30118
404 836–6419

HAWAII

University of Hawaii at Manoa
College of Business Administration
2530 Dole Street, C200
Hololulu, HI 96822

IDAHO

Boise State University
College of Business
1910 University Drive
Boise, ID 83725
208 385–1125

Idaho State University
College of Business
Box 8020
Pocatello, ID 83209
208 236–2135

ILLINOIS

Bradley University
College of Business
   Administration
Peoria, IL 61625
309 677–2253

DePaul University
College of Commerce
25 E. Jackson, Suite 1204
Chicago, IL 60604–2287

Illinois State University
College of Business
315 Williams Hall
Normal, IL 61761
309 438–2251

Loyola University of Chicago
Graduate School of Business
820 North Michigan Avenue
Chicago, IL 60611
312 915–6120

Northern Illinois University
College of Business
224 Wirtz Hall
De Kalb, IL 60115
815 753–1757

Northwestern University
J.L. Kellogg Graduate School of
   Management
2001 Sheridan Road
Evanston, IL 60208
708 491–3300

Southern Illinois University
   at Carbondale
College of Business &
   Administration
Carbondale, IL 62901–4620
618 453–3328

Southern Illinois University at
   Edwardsville
School of Business
Box 1051
Edwardsville, IL 62026
618 692–3822

University of Chicago
Graduate School of Business
1101 E. 58th Street
Chicago, IL 60637

University of Illinois at Chicago
College of Business
P.O. Box 4348
Chicago, IL 60680–2451
312 996–7000

University of Illinois at
  Urbana–Champaign
College of Commerce & Business
  Administration
319 Commerce West
1206 South Sixth Street
Champaign, IL 61820
217 333–4555

Western Illinois University
College of Business
Rm 101 Stipes Hall
Macomb, IL 61455
309 298–2442

INDIANA

Ball State University
College of Business
Graduate Business Programs,
  WB 146
Muncie, IN 47306
317 285–8192

Indiana State University
School of Business
951 Sycamore
Terre Haute, IN 47809
812 237–2000

Indiana University–Purdue
  University at Fort Wayne
School of Business & Management
  Sciences
Neff Hall Suite 330
Fort Wayne, IN 46805–1499

Indiana University at South Bend
Division of Business &
  Economics
1700 Mishawaka Avenue
P.O. Box 7111
South Bend, IN 46634
219 237–4217

Indiana University Bloomington
Graduate School of Business
10th and Fee Lane
School of Business 254
Bloomington, IN 47405
812 855–8006

Indiana University Northwest
Division of Business &
  Economics
3400 Broadway
Gary, IN 46408
219 980–6630

Purdue University
Krannert Graduate School of
  Management
Krannert Building
West Lafayette, IN 47907
317 494–9700

University of Notre Dame
College of Business Administration
133 Hayes Healy
Notre Dame, IN 46556
219 239–5000

IOWA

Drake University
College of Business & Public
  Administration
2507 University Avenue
Des Moines, IA 50311
515 271–2188

Iowa State University
College of Business
396 Carver Hall
Ames, IA 50011–2063
515 294–3656

University of Iowa
College of Business Administration
111 Phillips Hall
Iowa City, IA 52242
319 335–1037

KANSAS

Kansas State University
College of Business Administration
110 Calvin Hall
Manhattan, KS 66506
913 532–7190

University of Kansas
School of Business
203 Summerfield Hall
Lawrence, KS 66045
913 864–3795

Wichita State University
W. Frank Barton School of
  Business
Graduate Studies in Business
Box 48
Wichita, KS 67208
316 689–3200

KENTUCKY

Murray State University
College of Business & Public
  Affairs
University Station
Murray, KY 42071
502 762–4181

University of Kentucky
College of Business &
  Economics
Lexington, KY 40506–0034
606 257–3592

University of Louisville
School of Business
South Third Street
Louisville, KY 40292
502 588–6440

LOUISIANA

Louisiana State University &
  A&M College
College of Business Administration
Baton Rouge, LA 70803
504 388–3111

Louisiana State University in
  Shreveport
College of Business Administration
One University Place
Shreveport, LA 71115
318 797–5000

Louisiana Tech University
College of Administration &
  Business
P.O. Box 10318
Ruston, LA 71272
318 257–4528

Loyola University
Joseph A. Butt, S.J. College of
  Business Admin.
6363 St. Charles Avenue
New Orleans, LA 70118
504 865–3544

McNeese State University
College of Business
4100 Ryan Street
Lake Charles, LA 70609
318 475–5514

Nicholls State University
College of Business Administration
P.O. Box 2015, University Station
Thibodaux, LA 70310
504 446–8111

Northeast Louisiana University
College of Business Administration
Office of the Dean, CBA
Monroe, LA 71209–0100
318 342–1000

Southeastern Louisiana University
College of Business
P.O. Box 735, University Station
Hammond, LA 70402
504 549–2258

Tulane University
A.B. Freeman School of Business
New Orleans, LA 70118
504 286–5400

University of New Orleans
College of Business Administration
New Orleans, LA 70148
504 286–6241

MAINE

University of Maine
College of Business Administration
Stevens Hall
Orono, ME 04469–0158
207 581–1968

MARYLAND

Loyola College in Maryland
Joseph A. Sellinger School of
  Business & Management
4501 North Charles Street
Baltimore, MD 21210
410 323–1010

University of Baltimore
Robert G. Merrick School of
  Business
Charles at Mount Royal
Baltimore, MD 21201
301 625–3350

University of Maryland
Maryland Business School
MBA Office
Tydings Hall, Room 3014
College Park, MD 20742
301 454–2299

MASSACHUSETTS

Babson College
Babson Graduate School of
  Business
Babson Park
Wellesley, MA 02157–0310
617 239–1200

Bentley College
Graduate School
175 Forest Street
Waltham, MA 02154–4705
617 891–2108

Boston College
Wallace E. Carroll Graduate School
  of Management
140 Commonwealth Avenue
Fulton Hall 306
Chestnut Hill, MA 02167
617 552–8000

Boston University
Graduate School of Management
685 Commonwealth Avenue
Boston, MA 02215
617 353–2668

Clark University
Graduate School of Management
950 Main Street
Worcester, MA 01610
508 793–7406

Harvard University
Graduate School of Business
  Administration
Soldiers Field Road
Boston, MA 02163
617 495–6900

Massachusetts Institute of
  Technology
Sloan School of Management
50 Memorial Drive (E52–112)
Cambridge, MA 02139
617 253–2659

Northeastern University
College of Business Administration
360 Huntington Avenue
101 Hayden Hall
Boston, MA 02115
617 437–3232

Suffolk University
School of Management
8 Ashburton Place
Boston, MA 02108–2770
617 573–8307

University of Massachusetts
  at Amherst
School of Management
Amherst, MA 01003
413 545–5580

University of Massachusetts
  at Lowell
College of Management
1 University Avenue
Pasteur Hall
Lowell, MA 01854–9985
508 934–4000

MICHIGAN

Central Michigan University
School of Business Administration
Mount Pleasant, MI 48859

Eastern Michigan University
College of Business
300 W. Michigan Avenue
Ypsilanti, MI 48197

Michigan State University
Eli Broad Graduate School of
  Management
411 Eppley Center
East Lansing, MI 48824–1121

Oakland University
School of Business Administration
Room 417 Varner
Rochester, MI 48309–4401
313 370–3282

University of Detroit–Mercy
College of Business Administration
P.O. Box 19900
Detroit, MI 48219–3599
313 993–1202

University of Michigan
School of Business Administration
Ann Arbor, MI 48109–1234
313 764–1363

University of Michigan, Flint
School of Management
303 East Kearsley Street
Flint, MI 48502–2186
313 762–3160

Wayne State University
School of Business Administration
5201 Cass Avenue
Detroit, MI 48202
313 577–4510

Western Michigan University
Haworth College of Business
1201 Oliver Street
Kalamazoo, MI 49008
616 387–6060

MINNESOTA

St. Cloud University
College of Business
720 4th Avenue South
St. Cloud, MN 56301–4498
612 255–3212

University of Minnesota, Twin
  Cities
Curtis L. Carlson School of
  Management
271 19th Avenue South
#295 HHH
Minneapolis, MN 55455
612 625–0027

MISSISSIPPI

Millsaps College
Else School of Management
1701 N. State Street
Jackson, MS 39210
601 974–1000

Mississississipi State University
College of Business & Industry
P.O. Box Drawer 5288
Mississippi, MS 39762
601 325–2580

University of Mississippi
School of Business Administration
University, MS 38677
601 232–5820

University of Southern Mississippi
College of Business Administration
Southern Station, Box 5096
Hattiesburg, MS 39406–5096
601 266–4663

MISSOURI

Saint Louis University
School of Business &
  Administration
221 North Grand Boulevard
St. Louis, MO 63103
314 658–3800

University of Missouri, Columbia
College of Business & Public
  Administration
303 Middlebush Hall
Columbia, MO 65211
314 882–6688

University of Missouri, Kansas City
H.W. Bloch School of Business &
  Public Administration
5110 Cherry
Kansas City, MO 64110
816 235–2201

University of Missouri, St. Louis
School of Business Administration
8001 Natural Bridge Road
St. Louis, MO 63121
314 553–5881

Washington University
John M. Olin School of Business
One Brookings Drive
Campus Box 1133
St. Louis, MO 63130
314 935–6000

MONTANA

University of Montana
School of Business Administration
Missoula, MT 59812
406 243–4831

NEBRASKA

Creighton University
College of Business Administration
California Street at 24th Street
Omaha, NE 68178–0130
402 280–2850

University of Nebraska at Lincoln
College of Business Administration
14th & R Streets
Lincoln, NE 68588
402 472–3211

University of Nebraska at Omaha
College of Business
  Administration
60th & Dodge Streets
Room 414
Omaha, NE 68182
402 554–2303

NEVADA

University of Nevada, Las Vegas
Graduate College
4505 S. Maryland Parkway
Las Vegas, NV 89154
702 739–3362

University of Nevada, Reno
College of Business
  Administration
Reno, NV 89557
702 784–4912

NEW HAMPSHIRE

Dartmouth College
Amos Tuck School of Business
  Administration
100 Tuck Hall
Hanover, NH 03755–9040
603 646–2369

NEW JERSEY

Rutgers University
Graduate School of Management
92 New Street
Newark, NJ 07102
201 648–5128

Seton Hall University
W. Paul Stillman School of
  Business
400 South Orange Avenue
South Orange, NJ 07079
201 761–9013

NEW MEXICO

New Mexico State University
College of Business & Economics
Box 30001, Box 3AD
Las Cruces, NM 88003
505 646–2821

University of New Mexico
Robert O. Anderson Graduate
  School of Management
Albuquerque, NM 87131
505 277–6471

NEW YORK

Canisius College
Richard J. Wehle School of
  Business
2001 Main Street
Buffalo, NY 14208
716 883–7000

Clarkson University
School of Management
Potsdam, NY 13699–5770
315 268–6400

Columbia University
Columbia Business School
105 Uris Hall
New York, NY 10027

Cornell University
Samuel Curtis Johnson Graduate
  School of Management
303 Malott Hall
Ithaca, NY 14853
607 255–6418

CUNY Baruch College
School of Business & Public
  Administration
17 Lexington Avenue
Box 303
New York, NY 10010
212 447–3000

Fordham University
School of Business
East Fordham Road
New York, NY 10458
212 636–6000

Hofstra University
School of Business
Hempstead Turnpike
Hempstead, NY 11550
516 463–6600

New York University
Leonard N. Stern School of
  Business
100 Trinity Place
New York, NY 10006
212 285–6000

Rensselaer Polytechnic Institute
School of Management
Lally Management Center
Troy, NY 12180–3590
518 276–6802

Rochester Institute of Technology
College of Business
One Lomb Memorial Drive
Rochester, NY 14623–0887
716 475–2256

St. John's University
Graduate School of Business
  Administration
Grand Central & Utopia Parkways
Jamaica, NY 11439
718 990–6417

SUNY at Albany
School of Business
1400 Washington Avenue
Albany, NY 12222
518 442–4910

SUNY at Binghamton
School of Management
P.O. Box 6000
Binghamton, NY 13902–6000

SUNY at Buffalo
School of Management
Jacobs Management Center
Buffalo, NY 14260
716 636–3204

Syracuse University
School of Management
Syracuse, NY 13244

University of Rochester
Wm. E. Simon Graduate School of
  Business Administration
Dewey Hall
Rochester, NY 14627

NORTH CAROLINA

Appalachian State University
Walker College of Business
Boone, NC 28608
704 262–2057

Duke University
Fuqua School of Business
Towerview Road
FEDEX 134
Durham, NC 27706
919 660–7700

East Carolina University
School of Business
Greenville, NC 27858
919 757–6966

University of North Carolina at
  Chapel Hill
Kenan–Flagler Business School
CB #3490, Carroll Hall
Chapel Hill, NC 27599–3490
919 962–8301

University of North Carolina at
  Charlotte
Belk College of Business
  Administration
Charlotte, NC 28223
704 547–2213

University of North Carolina at
  Greensboro
Joseph M. Bryan School of
  Business & Economics
1000 Spring Garden Street
220 Bryan Building
Greensboro, NC 27412

Wake Forest University
Babcock Graduate School of
  Management
P.O. Box 7659 Reynolds Station
Winston–Salem, NC 27109
919 759–5421

Western Carolina University
Graduate Programs in Business
Forsyth Building
Cullowhee, NC 28723
704 227–7401

NORTH DAKOTA

University of North Dakota
College of Business Administration
P.O. Box 8098, University Station
Grand Forks, ND 58202
701 777–2135

OHIO

Bowling Green State University
College of Business Administration
Bowling Green, OH 43403
419 372–2747

Case Western Reserve University
Weatherhead School of
  Management
10900 Euclid Avenue
Cleveland, OH 44060
216 368–2030

Cleveland State University
James J. Nance College of Business
  Administration
Cleveland, OH 44115
216 687–3730

John Carroll University
School of Business
20700 North Park Boulevard
University Heights, OH 44118
216 397–4391

Kent State University
Graduate School of Management
Room 306 BSA
Kent, OH 44242–0001
216 672–2772

Miami University
School of Business Administration
Oxford, OH 45056
513 529–3631

Ohio State University
College of Business
1775 College Road
126 Hagerty Hall
Columbus, OH 43210
614 292–2715

Ohio University
College of Business Administration
106 Copeland Hall
Athens, OH 45701
614 593–2000

University of Akron
College of Business Administration
302 Buchtel Mall
Akron, OH 44325
216 972–7040

University of Cincinnati
College of Business Administration
Carl H. Lindner Hall, Suite 103
Cincinnati, OH 45221–0020
513 556–7002

University of Dayton
School of Business Administration
300 College Park Avenue
230 Miriam Hall
Dayton, OH 45469–2226
513 229–3733

University of Toledo
College of Business Administration
2801 West Bancroft
Toledo, OH 43606

Wright State University
College of Business &
  Administration
110 Rike Hall
Dayton, OH 45435
513 873–2437

OKLAHOMA

Oklahoma State University
College of Business Administration
Stillwater, OK 74078–0555
405 744–5064

University of Oklahoma
College of Business Administration
Norman, OK 73019
405 325–3611

University of Tulsa
College of Business Administration
600 South College
Tulsa, OK 74104
918 631–2213

OREGON

Oregon State University
College of Business
Corvallis, OR 97331
503 737–2551

Portland State University
School of Business Administration
P.O. Box 751
503 725–3712

University of Oregon
Graduate School of Management
College of Business
Eugene, OR 97403

University of Portland
School of Business Administration
5000 North Willamette Boulevard
Portland, OR 97203
503 283–7224

PENNSYLVANIA

Carnegie Mellon University
Graduate School of Industrial
  Administration
Tech & Frew Streets
Pittsburgh, PA 15213 3890
412 268–2268

Drexel University
College of Business &
  Administration
32nd & Chestnut Streets
Philadelphia, PA 19104
215 895–2110

Duquesne University
School of Business
600 Forbes Avenue
Pittsburgh, PA 15282

Lehigh University
College of Business & Economics
Bethlehem, PA 18015
215 758–4450

Pennsylvania State University
The Mary Jean & Frank P.
  Smeal College of Business
  Administration
801 Business Administration
  Building
University Park, PA 16802
814 863–0448

Temple University
School of Business & Management
Broad Street & Montgomery
  Avenue
Speakman Hall, Room 111
Philadelphia, PA 19122

University of Pennsylvania
The Wharton School
3620 Locust Walk
Philadelphia, PA 19104
215 898–3030

University of Pittsburgh
Joseph M. Katz Graduate School of
  Business
372 Mervis Hall, Roberto Clemente
  Drive
Pittsburgh, PA 15260
412 648–1500

Villanova University
College of Commerce & Finance
Villanova, PA 19085
215 645–4336

RHODE ISLAND

University of Rhode Island
College of Business Administration
Kingston, RI 02881–0802
401 792–5000

SOUTH CAROLINA

Clemson University
College of Commerce & Industry
201 Sikes Hall
Clemson, SC 29634

University of South Carolina
College of Business Administration
Columbia, SC 29208
803 777–3177

Winthrop College
School of Business Administration
204 Thurmond
Rock Hill, SC 29733
803 323–2186

SOUTH DAKOTA

University of South Dakota
School of Business
414 East Clark Street
Vermillion, SD 57069
605 677–5455

TENNESSEE

East Tennessee State University
College of Business
Johnson City, TN 37614
615 929–5489

Memphis State University
Fogelman College of Business &
  Economics
Memphis, TN 38152
901 678–2431

Middle Tennessee State University
College of Business
P.O. Box 115
Murfreesboro, TN 37132
615 898–2300

Tennessee Tech University
College of Business Development
Box 5023
Cookeville, TN 38505

University of Tennessee at
  Chattanooga
School of Business Administration
615 McCallie Avenue
Chattanooga, TN 37403
615 755–4313

University of Tennessee at
  Knoxville
Graduate School of Business
722A Stokely Management Center
Knoxville, TN 37996–0550
615 974–5033

Vanderbilt University
Owen Graduate School of
  Management
401 21st Avenue South
Nashville, TN 37203
615 322–2534

TEXAS

Baylor University
The Hankamer School of Business
P.O. Box 98001
Waco, TX 76798–8001
817 755–1211

East Texas State University
College of Business & Technology
East Texas Station
Commerce, TX 75429
903 886–5190

Lamar University
College of Business
P.O. Box 10059, Lamar U Station
Beaumont, TX 77710
409 880–8603

Southern Methodist University
Edwin L. Cox School of Business
Dallas, TX 75275–0333
214 692–3000

Stephen F. Austin State University
School of Business
1936 North Street
Nacogdoches, TX 75962
409 568–2011

Texas A&M University
College of Business Administration
601 Blocker Building
College Station, TX 77843–4113
409 845–4711

Texas Christian University
M.J. Neeley School of Business
2800 South University Drive
P.O. Box 32868
Fort Worth, TX 76129
817 921–7526

Texas Tech University
College of Business Administration
Lubbock, TX 79409
806 742–3188

University of Houston
College of Business Administration
4800 Calhoun Boulevard
Houston, TX 77004
713 749–2911

University of Houston–Clear Lake
School of Business & Public
  Administration
2700 Bay Area Boulevard
Houston, TX 77058

University of North Texas
College of Business Administration
P.O. Box 13737
Denton, TX 76203

University of Texas at Arlington
College of Business Administration
Box 19377
Arlington, TX 76019
817 273–3004

University of Texas at Austin
Graduate School of Business
GSB 2.104
Austin, TX 78712
512 471–5921

University of Texas at El Paso
College of Business Administration
500 West University Drive
El Paso, TX 79968
915 747–5241

University of Texas–Pan American
Graduate Business Program
1201 West University Drive
Edinburg, TX 78539
512 381–3311

University of Texas at San Antonio
College of Business
6900 N Loop 1604 W
San Antonio, TX 78249–0631
512 691–4313

UTAH

Brigham Young University
Marriott School of Management
640 Tanner Building
Provo, UT 84602
801 378–4121

University of Utah
David Eccles School of Business
Salt Lake City, UT 84112
801 581–7676

Utah State University
College of Business
UMC 3500
Logan, UT 84322
801 750–2360

VERMONT

University of Vermont
School of Business Administration
Burlington, VT 05405
802 656–4015

VIRGINIA

College of William & Mary
Graduate School of Business
Blow Memorial Hall
P.O. Box 8795
Williamsburg, VA 23187–8795
804 221–4100

George Mason University
School of Business Administration
4400 University Drive
Fairfax, VA 22030
703 993–1880

James Madison University
College of Business
Harrisonburg, VA 22807
703 568–6341

Old Dominion University
Graduate School of Business
  & Public Administration
Norfolk, VA 23529–0119
804 683–3520

University of Richmond
E.C. Robins School of Business
Richmond, VA 23173
804 289–8550

University of Virginia
Darden Graduate School of
  Business Administration
P.O. Box 6550
Charlottesville, VA 22906
804 924–3900

Virginia Commonwealth University
School of Business
901 West Franklin Street
Richmond, VA 23298
804 367–1741

Virginia Polytechnic Institute &
  State University
R.B. Pamplin College of Business
1044 Pamplin Hall
Blacksburg, VA 24061–0209
703 231–6601

WASHINGTON

Eastern Washington University
College of Business Administration
117 Showilter Hill
Cheney, WA 99004

Gonzaga University
School of Business Administration
Spokane, WA 99258–0001
509 328–4220

Pacific Lutheran University
School of Business Administration
Tacoma, WA 98447
206 535–7244

Seattle University
Albers School of Business &
  Economics
Broadway & Madison
Seattle, WA 98122
206 296–5700

University of Washington
Graduate School of Business
  Administration
110 Mackenzie Hall
Seattle, WA 98195
206 543–4750

Washington State University
College of Business & Economics
Todd Hall #473
Pullman, WA 99164–4744
509 335–7617

Western Washington University
College of Business & Economics
Bellingham, WA 98225–9072
206 676–3896

WEST VIRGINIA

West Virginia University
College of Business & Economics
P.O. Box 6025
Morgantown, WV 26506
304 293–5408

WISCONSIN

Marquette University
College of Business Administration
606 N. 13th Street
Milwaukee, WI 53233
414 288–7142

University of Wisconsin–La Crosse
College of Business Administration
1725 State Street
La Crosse, WI 54601
608 785–8000

University of Wisconsin–Madison
Graduate School of Business
1155 Observatory Drive
Madison, WI 53706
608 262–1553

University of Wisconsin–
  Milwaukee
School of Business Administration
P.O. Box 742
Milwaukee, WI 53201
414 229–4235

University of Wisconsin–Oshkosh
College of Business Administration
800 Algoma Boulevard
Oshkosh, WI 54901
414 424–1444

University of Wisconsin–
  Whitewater
College of Business & Economics
4037 Carlson Hall
Whitewater, WI 53190–1790
414 472–1343

WYOMING

University of Wyoming
College of Business
P.O. Box 3275
Laramie, WY 82071
307 766–2063